Moral Development: A Practical Guide for Jewish Teachers

By Earl Schwartz

ALTERNATIVES IN RELIGIOUS EDUCATION, INC.
DENVER, COLORADO

Published by
Alternatives in Religious Education, Inc.
3945 South Oneida Street
Denver, Colorado 80237

Library of Congress Catalog Number 83-70196

Printed in the United States of America

DEDICATION

To Nina

ACKNOWLEDGEMENTS

These materials were composed and assembled over a period of four years. During that time I received the generous help of many friends and co-workers including: the staff and students of the Talmud Torah of St. Paul; the staff and children of Community Child Care, Inc.; Ruti Gavish, my wise and dear friend; and Audrey Friedman Marcus and Rabbi Raymond A. Zwerin.

I'd also like to thank the Harry Rosenthal Educational Fund for its financial support of the project. Mr. and Mrs. Rosenthal's personal interest in moral education provided the initial impetus for the preparation of these materials.

Finally, thanks to Rabbi Joel Gordon for his help and support. His assistance, both personal and professional, has been invaluable.

TABLE OF CONTENTS

INTRODUCTION

One Sunday morning, a few years back, I told a group of nine and ten year olds the famous story of how Hillel, unable to pay for his daily Torah lesson, listened to the lecture through a skylight (*Yoma* 35b). I chose the story because I felt that Hillel's actions were a wonderful expression of devotion to *talmud Torah*. I assumed that Hillel's behavior could not help but evoke each listener's empathy. You can therefore imagine my surprise when, on this particular morning, the empathy I evoked was rather tepid. In fact, I soon found myself scrambling to defend Hillel against a volley of accusations. Instead of seeing Hillel as a model of piety, several students derided him as a cheat and a coward who had "ripped off" a lesson via the skylight. In their eyes, Hillel was no better than someone who sneaks into a movie theater through the exit. I left class quite befuddled. How could I have so grossly miscalculated my students' reaction to the story?

About a year before giving this lesson about Hillel, I had begun work on this dilemma-discussion moral development curriculum for use in Jewish schools. The curriculum is in large part based upon the research of Dr. Lawrence Kohlberg, Professor of Education and Social Psychology at Harvard. Kohlberg's theory of moral development proposes that:

1. "... there is a natural sense of justice intuitively known by the child."[1]
2. "... moral judgment develops through ... [a] culturally universal invariant sequence of stages."[2]
3. "... the existence of moral stages ... provide[s] a universal or non-relative and non-arbitrary approach to moral education. They define the aim of moral education as that of stimulating movement to the next stage of moral development ... the process for doing this ... rests on having students discuss moral dilemmas in such a way that they confront the limits of their reasoning and that of their fellow students."[3]
4. "One important stimulus to moral development is ... the sense of uncertainty which arises when one's easy judgments lead to contradiction of uncertainty when facing difficult decisions. A second stimulus is exposure to the next stage of reasoning above one's own."[4]

On the basis of these four principles, Kohlberg maintains that moral judgment develops through a set series of stages. Each of these stages is typical of a particular period in one's overall maturation, but they are not strictly correlated with specific ranges of age. This is because moral development is also a learning process: one must acquire, stage by stage, ever more adequate structures of moral logic. Kohlberg's research suggests that this type of learning is achieved through the thoughtful consideration of moral dilemmas.

Through the first year of developing my curriculum, I had yet to witness a dramatic confirmation of Kohlberg's findings. Now, as I mulled over what might have been behind the lack of empathy on the part of my class for Hillel, it occurred to me that the confirmation I was looking for might perhaps be staring me in the face. The lesson on Hillel had, in fact, turned into a discussion of a moral dilemma, posing the question: Is simple egalitarianism always an adequate measure of justice? Perhaps I had expected of my students a moral judgment for which they were cognitively unprepared.

To test my hypothesis, the story about Hillel was transformed into a dilemma about a child who is confined to a wheelchair and is thus barred from attending school by architectural, rather than financial, barriers. I wanted to see if my class would empathize with such a child any more than they had with Hillel. Specifically, I asked the class whether money which had been set aside for use by the student body as a whole should be used to make the necessary architectural changes for this one new child. At first, the discussion of the "new" story followed the same line of reasoning with which poor Hillel had been "done in." But at a crucial point in the discussion, two concepts were introduced that turned the whole thing around.

First, one student was unable to maintain his argument against making the architectural changes when I asked him whether the child in the wheelchair had a *right* to attend the school. On the tail of this impasse, another student wondered aloud whether the *brit* at Sinai, which mandated that *talmud Torah* be made available to *all* Jewish children, was more important than simple "fairness." The second child was actually struggling to apply the concept of rights to this dilemma. With this concept at their disposal, several of the students came to see the dilemma in a very different light. Before the idea of rights was introduced into the discussion, most of the students did not have the conceptual tools necessary to understand the virtue of Hillel's behavior. When these tools were provided, those who were prepared to do so quickly scampered forward a bit in moral judgment. At the end of the discussion, I was convinced that I had witnessed what Kohlberg's cognitive-developmental theory predicts: the development of moral judgment through guided exploration of a moral dilemma.

The Dilemma-Discussion Model in Traditional Jewish Sources

Examples of teaching ethical principles through moral dilemmas are found throughout Jewish literature. Rabbinic sources make frequent use of the dilemma-discussion model (e.g.,*Baba Metzia* 1a: If two people grab an abandoned article at exactly the same time, to whom does the article belong? and *Ketubot* 17a: May one take liberties with the truth to spare another's feelings?). In *Tanach* such discussions often flow from a dilemma over which God and a prophet meet in dialogue. Abraham's attempt to save Sodom (Genesis 18), the case of the daughters of Zelophehad (Numbers 27, 36) and chapter four of the book of Jonah (note how it ends with a question) are all examples of this process.

In many of these dialogues the participants' lines of reasoning are quite explicit. In the discussion between God and Abraham about the fate of Sodom, for instance, Abraham uses a *kal va-homer* argument (an inference from a less important to a more important matter) when he says, "Will the Judge of all the earth not do justice?" to secure God's commitment to spare the innocent. Another such discussion in which a *kal va-homer* argument plays a significant role comes in the wake of Miriam's bout with leprosy (Numbers 12). Here Miriam is affected with the disease for showing disrespect towards her brother Moses. Moses, being the most humble of all people (Numbers 12:3), is *mohel al k'vodo* (humble and self-effacing) and thus prays for Miriam's immediate recovery. The Lord, however, suggests to Moses that if his intercession were immediately successful, it would seem as though Moses could be taunted with impunity. This, in turn, would undermine the authority of both God and Moses. God nails down the point with a *kal va-homer* argument: If a similar act of disrespect towards a parent deserves punishment, how much the more so when it is directed towards "My servant Moses" (Numbers 12:7,8).

But the most dramatic and complete example of the dilemma-discussion method found in Jewish sources is the confrontation between Nathan and David in II Samuel, chapter 12. Here we have it all: an actual dilemma (David has Uriah disposed of and takes Bathsheba as his wife) transformed into a hypothetical problem (the poor man and his lamb), an initial reaction to the dilemma (David's exclamation: "Someone who would do that deserves death!"), guidance from a morally superior source (Nathan's reply: "You are that man!") and moral advancement (David's admission: "I have sinned against the Lord").

Three Possible Problems

We have seen how the dilemma-discussion model is frequently found in the classic Jewish sources, but three important questions remain to be considered before the method can be prescribed for use in our schools:

1. Does the dilemma-discussion method threaten the norm-setting authority of the traditional sources?
2. To what extent do the stages of moral development, which Kohlberg has derived from his cross-cultural research, correspond with a classic Jewish hierarchy of values?
3. Does this method make a connection between *knowing* what is right and *doing* what is right? Let us consider each of these questions individually.

Does the dilemma-discussion method threaten the norm-setting authority of the traditional sources? Consider a comment by R. Saadya Gaon in this regard: "... we inquire and speculate in matters of our religion for two reasons: (1) in order that we may actualize what we know in the way of imparted knowledge from the prophets of God, and (2) in order that we may be able to refute those who attack us on matters connected with our religion. For our Lord (be He blessed and exalted) instructed us in everything that we require in the way of religion, through the intermediacy of the prophets ... He also informed us that by speculation and inquiry we shall attain to certainty on every point in accordance with the truth revealed through the words of His messenger."[5]

Saadya presages modern cognitivists like Kohlberg when he maintains that a concept is not fully "actualized" unless it is rationally integrated into one's existing thought structure. Saadya can therefore confidently assert that teachers of Torah have nothing to fear from rational inquiry.

Bahya Ibn Pakudah, in his classic *Duties of the Heart* (*Chovot HaLivavot*), shared Saadya's cognitivist orientation. Commenting on the passage, "Is this how you intend to requite the Lord, O foolish and unwise nation? ... remember way back, think over the ancient past, ask your father and he will tell you..." (Deuteronomy 32:6-7). Bahya asserts: "This serves as a proof of what we previously stated, i.e., that though it be natural that one first learn from tradition, there is no good reason why someone who is able to clarify his own thinking through logic should rely on [tradition] alone, for it is mandatory that one reflect upon those things which can be grasped by way of the intellect, and to formulate logical proofs through the use of reason if one has the ability to do so."[6]

Rav Hama bar Hanina saw an allusion to the value of dialectical learning in the verse, "As iron sharpens iron, so one person sharpens the face of another" (Proverbs 27:17). "Rav Hama bar Hanina said that this means that just as one piece of iron sharpens another, so too do *talmiday chachamim* sharpen one another in matters of *halachah*" (*Yalkut Shimoni* On Proverbs 27:17). Indeed, the speculations that pass between teacher and student are the heartbeat of the living Torah, as in the Rabbinic dictum: "Even that which an advanced student points out to his teacher sometime in the future, has already been told to Moses at Sinai."[7]

The central element of each unit in this book is a dilemma story. However, each unit also includes a collection of references from traditional sources which touch upon the particular value concept at stake in the dilemma. These traditional sources are not meant to be used simultaneously with the dilemma-discussion portion of the unit, as this might cut short the process of inquiry which we seek to encourage. Rather, the sources are meant to be used by teachers sometime after the initial discussion to guide and reinforce the students' own judgment. The curriculum *does* presuppose a set hierarchy of Jewish values (as is expressed in the traditional sources), but is built on the assumption that it is preferable for students to develop an understanding of the function and need for these values (in Saadya's terms, to "actualize" them), rather than simply to present Jewish values as a "bag of virtues." By a "bag of virtues," Kohlberg refers to a set of personality traits generally considered to be positive.[8]

To what extent do the stages of moral development which Kohlberg has derived from his cross-cultural research correspond with a classic Jewish hierarchy of values? In the chart below are passages from two sources. The first is Kohlberg's six stages of moral reasoning. Note that each stage has a distinct cognitive basis for moral judgments. The second is a selection from Maimonides' *Mishnah Commentary*. Here, too, we have a series of cognitive-developmental stages, with each stage characterized by a particular type of rationale for doing *mitzvot*.

The Six Stages of Moral Judgment

Level A. Preconventional Level

Stage 1. The Stage of Punishment and Obedience

Content

Right is literal obedience to rules and authority, avoiding

punishment, and not doing physical harm.

1. What is right is to avoid breaking rules, to obey for obedience sake, and to avoid doing physical damage to people and property.
2. The reasons for doing right are avoidance of punishment and the superior power of authorities.

Social Perspective

This stage takes an egocentric point of view. A person at this stage doesn't consider the interests of others or recognize they differ from actor's, and doesn't relate two points of view. Actions are judged in terms of physical consequences rather than in terms of psychological interests of others. Authority's perspective is confused with one's own.

Stage 2. The Stage of Individual Instrumental Purpose and Exchange

Content

Right is serving one's own or other's needs and making fair deals in terms of concrete exchange.

1. What is right is following rules when it is to someone's immediate interest. Right is acting to meet one's own interests and needs and letting others do the same. Right is also what is fair; that is, what is an equal exchange, a deal, an agreement.
2. The reason for doing right is to serve one's own needs or interests in a world where one must recognize that other people have their interests, too.

Social Perspective

This stage takes a concrete individualistic perspective. A person at this stage separates own interests and points of view from those of authorities and others. He or she is aware everybody has individual interests to pursue and these conflict, so that right is relative (in the concrete individualistic sense). The person integrates or relates conflicting individual interests to one another through instrumental exchange of services, through instrumental need for the other and the other's goodwill, or through fairness giving each person the same amount.

Level B. Conventional Level

Stage 3. The Stage of Mutual Interpersonal Expectations, Relationships, and Conformity

Content

The right is playing a good (nice) role, being concerned about the other people and their feelings, keeping loyalty and trust with partners, and being motivated to follow rules and expectations.

1. What is right is living up to what is expected by people close to one or what people generally expect of people in one's role as son, sister, friend, and so on. "Being good" is important and means having good motives, showing concern about others. It also means keeping mutual relationships, maintaining trust, loyalty, respect, and gratitude.
2. Reasons for doing right are needing to be good in one's own eyes and those of others, caring for others, and because if one puts oneself in the other person's place one would want good behavior from the self (Golden Rule).

Social Perspective

This stage takes the perspective of the individual in relationship to other individuals. A person at this stage is aware of shared feelings, agreements, and expectations, which take primacy over individual interests. The person relates points of view through the "concrete Golden Rule," putting oneself in the other person's shoes. He or she does not consider generalized "system" perspective.

Stage 4. The Stage of Social System and Conscience Maintenance

Content

The right is doing one's duty in society, upholding the social order, and maintaining the welfare of society or the group.

1. What is right is fulfilling the actual duties to which one has agreed. Laws are to be upheld except in extreme cases where they conflict with other fixed social duties and rights. Right is also contributing to society, the group, or institution.
2. The reasons for doing right are to keep the institution going as a whole, set respect or conscience as meeting one's defined obligations, or the consequence "What if everyone did it?"

Social Perspective

This stage differentiates societal point of view from interpersonal agreement or motives. A person at this stage takes the viewpoint of the system which defines roles and rules. He or she considers individual relations in terms of place in the system.

Level B/C. Transitional Level

This level is postconventional but not yet principled.

Content of Transition

At Stage 4½, choice is personal and subjective. It is based on emotions, conscience is seen as arbitrary and relative, as are ideas such as "duty" and "morally right."

Transitional Social Perspective

At this stage, the perspective is that of an individual standing outside of his own society and considering himself as an individual making decisions without a generalized commitment or contract with society. One can pick and choose obligations, which are defined by particular societies, but one has no principles for such choice.

Level C. Postconventional and Principled Level

Moral decisions are generated from rights, values, or principles that are (or could be) agreeable to all individuals composing or creating a society designed to have fair and beneficial practices.

Stage 5. The Stage of Prior Rights and Social Contract or Utility

Content

The right is upholding the basic rights, values, and legal contracts of a society, even when they conflict with the concrete rules and laws of the group.

1. What is right is being aware of the fact that people hold a variety of values and opinions, that most values and rules are relative to one's group. These "relative" rules should usually be upheld, however, in the interest of impartiality and because they are the social contract. Some nonrelative values and rights such as life, and liberty, however, must be upheld in any society and regardless of majority opinion.
2. Reasons for doing right are, in general, feeling obligated to obey the law because one has made a social contract to make and abide by laws for the good of all and to protect their own rights and the rights of others. Family, friendship, trust, and work obligations are also commitments or contracts freely entered into and entail respect for the rights of others. One is concerned that laws and duties be based on rational calculation of overall utility: "the greatest good for the greatest number."

Social Perspective

This stage takes a prior-to-society perspective — that of a

rational individual aware of values and rights prior to social attachments and contracts. The person integrates perspectives by formal mechanisms of agreement, contract, objective impartiality, and due process. He or she considers the moral point of view and the legal point of view, recognizes they conflict, and finds it difficult to integrate them.

Stage 6. The Stage of Universal Ethical Principles

Content

This stage assumes guidance by universal ethical principles that all humanity should follow.

1. Regarding what is right, Stage 6 is guided by universal ethical principles. Particular laws or social agreements are usually valid because they rest on such principles. When laws violate these principles, one acts in accordance with the principle. Principles are universal principles of justice: the equality of human rights and respect for the dignity of human beings as individuals. These are not merely values that are recognized, but are also principles used to generate particular decisions.
2. The reason for doing right is that, as a rational person, one has seen the validity of principles and has become committed to them.

Social Perspective

This stage takes the perspective of a moral point of view from which social arrangements derive or on which they are grounded. The perspective is that of any rational individual recognizing the nature of morality or the basic moral premise of respect for other persons as ends, not means.

"The Six Stages of Moral Judgment," Appendix, pages 409-12 from THE PHILOSOPHY OF MORAL DEVELOPMENT: Moral Stages and the Idea of Justice by Lawrence Kohlberg. Essays on Moral Development, Volume I. Copyright ©1981 by Lawrence Kohlberg. By permission of Harper & Row, Publishers, Inc.

Mishnah Commentary[9]

Imagine a child who is brought to a teacher to teach him Torah. This is actually the most important element in his development, but because he is young and intellectually weak he doesn't understand its value and how it will contribute to his development. Therefore, the teacher (who is more developed than he) is forced to motivate him to study through things which he does find desirable, as befits his young age. So he [the teacher] says, "Read, and I'll give you some nuts and dates, and I'll give you a little honey," and for this he reads and makes an effort — not for the sake of the reading itself, because he doesn't appreciate its value, but rather, so that he can get the food. Eating these sweets is more valuable to him than reading, and certainly much superior to it, so he considers studying a burdensome chore which he's willing to put up with in order to get the desired result: a nut or a little honey.

When he grows and his intellect becomes stronger and he thus loses interest in the thing which had previously been important to him and is no longer obsessed with it, you have to motivate him through something that he *does* find desirable. So his teacher says to him, "Read, and I'll get you some nice shoes or some attractive clothes," and for this he'll try to read, not for the sake of the study itself, but for the clothing, which is more important to him than the Torah, and which is therefore his reason for reading.

When he's more intellectually developed he'll come to think lightly of this as well and will then set his heart on something superior to it, and thus his teacher will say, "Learn this passage or chapter and I will give you a dinar or two," and for that he'll read and make the effort — to get the money. That money is more important to him than the study, because the purpose of studying is to get the money that was promised to him for it.

When he becomes quite knowledgeable and he doesn't think much of this [the money] because he knows that it's really of little value, he will desire something more worthwhile, and so his teacher will say to him, "Learn this so that you can become a head of the community and a judge. People will respect you and stand up when you go by, like so and so." So he'll read and make the effort, so that he might reach this rank. His purpose will be to gain respect and praise from others.

But all of this is unbecoming ... our sages have warned us that one should not have some ulterior motive in serving God and doing a *mitzvah* ... Antigonos of Socho said, "Don't be like servants who serve the master so that they might receive a reward, but rather, like servants who serve the master even though they don't receive a reward." What I mean to say is that one should believe the truth for the sake of its truth, and this is what is called "service out of love."

In comparing these two sets of stages, we see that Maimonides and Kohlberg agree that:

1. Reasoning is an essential part of moral behavior.

2. Human beings pass through stages of moral development.
3. There is *some* correspondence between *age* and *stage*.
4. The thrust of moral development is *from* physical rewards, *through* "good roles," *to* principled behavior.

Maimonides is only one authority on the matter, but he is an exceedingly important one. The striking similarity between these two taxonomies suggests that Kohlberg's hierarchy of values is essentially compatible with a classic Jewish value structure.

Does the dilemma-discussion method fail to connect knowing what is right with doing what is right? In an address to the National Catholic Education Association in 1975, Kohlberg made the rather daring assertion that the gap between having moral principles and acting upon them is bridged by "faith." The fact that people who had reached the highest stage of moral development also tended to be people who were "deeply religious" led him to concur with James Fowler's hypotheses (*Stages of Faith,* 1981) that there is a series of "faith stages" which runs roughly parallel to his own set of moral stages. Kohlberg concluded that these two sets of stages complement one another: "Moral principles ... do not require faith for their formulation or for their justification. In some sense, however, to ultimately live up to moral principles requires faith. For this reason, we believe, the ultimate exemplars of Stage 6 morality also appear to be men of faith."[10]

This formulation of faith as that which empowers us to act on our principles is very close to the biblical notion of *emunah. Emunah* is the strength we draw from one another, and ultimately from God, to persist in our pursuit of what is right and good. Here "faith" is not the substance of our values, but rather, the state of mind and spirit that allows for their fulfillment, developing parallel to the values we may hold at any given stage. A teacher of moral principles must therefore not only be concerned with a student's *cognitive* moral development, but must also nourish that student's existential sense of *emunah*. The teacher of Torah should strive to be like Moses *our* teacher, *ne'eman,* a model of faithfulness to persons and principles. In this way we may help to enlarge our students' range of *emunah*.

The paradigm, then, is: *talmud* + *emunah* ⟶ *ma'aseh,* which brings to mind the famous *baraita*: "When Rabbi Tarfon and the sages were dining in the upper chamber of the house of Nitzah in Lydda, this question was asked to them: 'What is greater, study or practice?' Rabbi Tarfon answered, 'Practice is greater.' Rabbi Akiba answered, 'Study is greater.' Then all the sages said, 'Study is greater because study leads to practice.'"[11]

Lawrence Kohlberg's work has been the subject of an enormous amount of criticism. His theory of developmental stages has been attacked as inflexible and arbitrary, but the fact that both the form and content of the approach is sound from a Jewish point of view renders much of this criticism irrelevant to Jewish education. It seems clear that discussions of dilemmas, in and of themselves, cannot transform people into paragons of virtue. Even after acquiring a rational appreciation of a certain value, a person must be sustained by "good faith" if he/she is to act in keeping with that understanding. This is especially the case when there are strong influences pushing one to act to the contrary. But the need for *emunah* does not cancel out the need for understanding (*havanah*). In a *talmid chacham, emunah* and *havanah* work hand in hand.

Kohlberg's Six Stages

You will recall that Kohlberg identifies six basic stages of moral development. Each of these stages is characterized by a particular sort of moral reasoning, and movement through these stages is understood as both a maturational and a learning process. In Stage 1, for instance, moral judgments tend to be made on the basis of obedience vs. punishment, whereas in Stage 2, they are oriented towards "satisfying the self's needs."

From ages seven through fourteen, most children reason in ways which are characteristic of Kohlberg's middle stages: 2, 3, and 4 (5 and 6 are mostly post-adolescent stages; Stage 1 is typical of early childhood). There are formal tests available for ascertaining students levels of moral reasoning, but informed observation of a few preliminary dilemma-discussions should give a teacher a very good sense of the class members' predominant stages of reasoning.

The purpose of this taxonomy is often misunderstood. One common misconception is that the taxonomy describes types of people. This is a very unfortunate point of confusion. Kohlberg's stages describe moral premises and lines of reasoning, *not* types of people. A second common misunderstanding of Kohlberg's work is the assumption that a person's moral reasoning must fit into precisely one stage at any given time. In fact, Kohlberg's findings tend to suggest that one's moral judgment is a *composite* of *previous, predominant* and *anticipated* stages. In light of these two points, what then is the educational value of Kohlberg's taxonomy?

Kohlberg's categorization of types of moral reasoning is educationally valuable to the extent that it suggests what type of reasoning a given student will find most developmentally challenging. The taxonomy helps us as teachers to ask our students the right questions, questions which are within "walking distance" of the students' present cognitive structure. You can bring a Stage 5 line of reasoning into a Stage 2 argument, but it will leave no permanent structural tracks for the student to trace back to Stage 5. Moral challenges are most effective when they are "local," i.e., from the next highest stage, and the taxonomy can serve as a road map in this regard.

How to Choose or Compose a Dilemma Story

With the information above clearly in mind, teachers can decide which kinds of dilemmas are most appropriate for their classes. For instance, a dilemma which simply poses the question of whether pure accidents and intentional acts are morally equal will not be developmentally challenging for a child who usually reasons at Stage 4, since a moral appreciation of intentionality is achieved at Stage 3. Likewise, the use of a dilemma which can *only* be understood as centering on a conflict between contract and conscience would be developmentally premature, and therefore ineffective, for a group which is most at home in a Stage 3 values structure.

Kohlberg defines a moral dilemma as "a state of social disequilibrium characterized by the unresolved conflicting claims of individuals." Stories revolving around such a state of "social disequilibrium" can be obtained from a variety of sources. When looking for potential dilemma stories, the most important question to ask is: will the students who hear this story be able to recognize that resolving the problem it poses requires that they evaluate and prioritize the relative moral validity of the conflicting claims the story presents?

Much of *Tanach* deals with "unresolved claims" and "social disequilibrium." Joab's decision to kill Absalom (II Samuel 18), Michal and Jonathan's decision to help David escape from Saul (I Samuel 19, 20), Abraham's decision to go ahead with the *Akedah* (Genesis 22), and Jephthah's decision to fulfill his vow (Judges 11), each follows upon the presentation of a powerful moral dilemma. Biblical narratives like these can be used as dilemmas by having your students decide upon the best course of action for the narrative's central character before going on to analyze the choice that character actually made. Using the *Tanach* in this way not only helps to develop moral judgment — it is also sound and stimulating Bible study!

Basal readers and literature texts can also be a source of dilemma stories. In addition, several sets of ready-made dilemmas are now available, including a set of filmstrips which Kohlberg helped to produce (see Bibliography).

You may also choose to compose your own dilemmas. Writing your own dilemmas allows you to tailor the stories to the specific needs and experiences of your class. I have already mentioned how the story of Hillel was transformed into a dilemma about a child in a wheelchair. That dilemma is now part of a unit in this curriculum. The dilemmas in this book will serve as models to help you create or adapt stories for dilemmas of your own.

Whether you choose to use dilemmas which have been written by others or decide to compose your own, bear in mind the following suggestions:

1. Try to avoid characterizations which the students might understand stereotypically. Characters engaged in questionable activities should not be gratuitously stigmatized. Once, in the course of evaluating a dilemma that I had written, a reviewer noticed that Teutonic names were used for every dubious character in the story, names which might sound particularly harsh to Jewish ears. One researcher who used filmstrips to present her dilemmas found that a particular group of students was seriously distracted from the actual dilemma by the color of one of the characters (although this, of course, is a moral dilemma in its own right).
2. Try to avoid characterizations which strongly suggest individuals with whom the students are personally acquainted. Recognizing a character makes it much more difficult to be objective about that character's role in the dilemma.
3. A well-crafted narrative makes for an easier presentation of the dilemma. Too many extraneous details can be distracting. Unless such details are an integral part of the story or being considered from a literary point of view, it's probably best to skip them.
4. The dilemma should end with a clear and relatively specific question concerning one of the character's actions, e.g., "Should David take the money?", "Did Sandra do the right thing?", etc.

Leading a Discussion of a Dilemma

An earlier comment noted that it is preferable for a class which is discussing a moral dilemma to be made up of members who are *not* all at exactly the same level of moral reasoning. This is because exposure to reasoning one step higher than one's own is a crucial element in the development of moral judgment. When a few articulate class members come up with a solution to a dilemma which is one step above the position of the majority, the discussion will contain the type of cognitive tension which Kohlberg has identified as a highly significant factor in moral development. Thus, if you find that your students all tend to employ the same line of reasoning in solving a particular dilemma, it becomes your responsibility to introduce this tension into the discussion. It is clearly preferable that this process be the product of differences between peers, but when students are all in agreement, the task of suggesting a higher stage solution to the dilemma falls to the teacher. Yet, we must be careful in this regard not simply to bulldoze the discussion toward a higher stage solution. The dilemma-discussion method emphasizes growth in reasoning and this takes time and tact. It is important that a dilemma be looked at from many different angles so that no one leaps to artificial, unreasoned solutions. During this process of fully sizing up the dilemma, there should be adequate opportunity for the teacher to hint at, probe for, or, as a last resort, suggest a higher stage solution. The first and most important principle in the procedure is simply to challenge every conclusion with "Why — *mai tama*?"

Here, for instance, is a portion of a conversation I had with three twelve-year-olds concerning dilemma number eight of this curriculum, entitled "*Revenge*":

Me: For those who said, "Tell her it's her own fault and you won't give it back to her" — I'd like to hear one person tell me why you said that.

S.F.: Because she did it to me and I think she should learn how it feels ... I mean, you should treat others like they want you to treat them, and if she wants to treat us her way then I'll treat her back.

Me: What would be the benefit of doing the same thing to her that she's done to you?

S.F.: There wouldn't be.

Me: You would do it simply because she made you angry?

S.F.: (Nods head in agreement)

Me: Who gave answer #3 — that they would ignore her? (E.S. raises hand). Why?

E.S.: Because I wouldn't want to get involved with her ... Because she might blame you for hiding her bag or something, and she just might — I don't know — I just wouldn't want to get involved ...

Me: Don't you have a responsibility to give it back?

E.S.: Well, I didn't *hide* it, so ...

Me: Somebody who said, "Give her back the bag?" S.K., Why?

S.K.: Because I don't think it would do anything. She'd probably still do stuff and let me get blamed for it. If I thought that she was so rotten for doing all that, I wouldn't want myself to do things that she did because I would be just as bad as her.

Me: Wouldn't you be encouraging her by giving her her bag when she asked?

S.K.: Well, sort of, but ...

Analysis of this series of exchanges suggests that S.F. is most concerned about the need to give a "non-reciprocator" a taste of her own medicine, while E.S. and S.K. seem to be more concerned about how they can avoid becoming contaminated with "badness." In response to my question concerning the function of revenge, S.F. insists upon retribution for its own sake as the only fitting treatment for someone who doesn't respect the golden rule of reciprocity, or should we say, S.F.'s rather charming version of that rule. E.S. and S.K., on the other hand, virtually ignore the question of reciprocity, focusing instead on how to get through the dilemma without themselves becoming "bad." If you refer back to Kohlberg's taxonomy, you'll see that S.F. appears to be pursuing a line of reasoning which is characteristic of Stage 2 (emphasis on naive reciprocity), while E.S. and S.K. appear to be reasoning near Stage 3 (good boy/good girl orientation). This being the case, the teacher's job for the balance of the discussion is to make sure that either the teacher or another student challenge S.F. with reasoning typical of Stage 3 (E.S. and S.K.'s line of reasoning), while at the same time, if possible, providing E.S. and S.K. with an example of reasoning at Stage 4 ("What is your duty in this situation? What are the social consequences of your position? What if everyone did what you're proposing?").

One other important point about dilemma-discussions: it is very easy to get sidetracked. For this reason you may sometimes wish to provide your students with a limited number of solutions to the dilemma. This might seem to be an unwarranted restriction on the free exercise of their reasoning skills, but it can help to prevent them from inventing ways of slipping out of the dilemma without really confronting the problem. Try to provide at least one choice which is typical of the majority of your students' stage of reasoning and one choice which is typical of the stage that comes after it.

How to Conclude a Dilemma Discussion

Most of the dilemmas in this collection have been designed for an initial presentation-discussion period of approximately 45 minutes. (Exceptions are: Unit I, which is divided into three 15 minute sub-units, and Unit XIII, which is designed for two 45 minute sessions.) Although there are no hard and fast rules as to when it is best to end a dilemma-discussion, it is probably about time to conclude a discussion if any of the following things are happening:

1. Several minutes have passed with no new ideas having been introduced into the discussion (by either the teacher or the students).
2. Everyone seems to have reached an equilibrium in terms of their respective positions on the issue.
3. Many students are no longer participating in the discussion or actively listening to it.

A good rule of thumb is that it is better to end a session while the discussion is still active than to have it stretch beyond its productive limits. Discussions which are interrupted while they are still vigorous can easily be reactivated later, but an artificially prolonged session may turn sour.

Here are some suggestions on how to wind up a discussion session:

1. Review the major points brought up during the course of the discussion.
2. Encourage the students to continue to think over the arguments they heard during the discussion. Suggest that they discuss the dilemma with their friends and family.
3. Suggest that the discussion be continued during future class sessions if anyone comes up with a new perspective on the issue or a new argument to bolster his or her position.

Evaluation of a Dilemma-Discussion Unit

In evaluating a dilemma-discussion moral development unit, it is important to keep in mind that the focal point of the approach is the development of *moral reasoning*. This means that it is not the students' immediate expression of appreciation for a particular value which validates the approach but, rather, the observation of long-term development in the way the students think about moral questions. This sort of development can only be spotted in the context of subsequent discussions. Traditional sources, whether biblical, *aggadic*, or *halachic*, can be very useful in this regard. A discussion of a point of *halachah* which is related to a previous dilemma may provide the teacher with a sense of how well the students have integrated the new moral schema into their own thought structures. For instance, an important Stage 3 concept is "intentionality." Following up a dilemma on intentionality with a discussion of the Rabbinic dictum: "*Mitzvot* must be intended" (*Berachot* 13a) may give a teacher a good idea of how deeply the dilemma has "sunk in." Remember, however, that this type of evaluation will be most revealing if the passage of several intervening lessons obscures the connection between the initial dilemma and the follow-up discussion.

Is There More Than One Type of Principled Reasoning?

In recent years several researchers in the field of moral and religious development have suggested that there exists a developmental track based on "responsible love" (Greek: *agape*; Hebrew: *middat chasidim*) which complements and, perhaps in some cases, supercedes a Stage 6 ethic of justice (Shawver 1979; Gilligan 1977). Carol Gilligan, a psychologist and former co-worker of Kohlberg's, has recently published research which suggests that women, once beyond the middle stages in Kohlberg's taxonomy, tend to continue their development along the lines of personal love and responsibility, rather than assimilating an ethic based on universal principles of justice. Does this mean that there is more than one type of principled moral reasoning?

It is Kohlberg's contention that, properly speaking, "responsible love" describes a *faith attitude*, not a principle. He maintains, however, that in its most highly developed form, such love presupposes Stage 6 principles of justice: "... although an ethic of agape goes beyond justice to supererogation, it still requires principles of fairness to resolve justice dilemmas ... Acts of agape cannot be demanded or expected by their recipients but are, rather acts of grace from the standpoint of the recipient."[12]

Kohlberg goes on to conclude that Gilligan's research has picked up on an aspect of human growth much broader than the development of moral reasoning: "We do not deny the possibility that research on the resolution of dilemmas differing from our own might validly lead to different stage definitions from those suggested by our research on justice dilemmas. Such stages, however, we would construe as stages in the development of a broader ethic or valuing process such as Fowler has attempted to describe. Such an ethic or valuing process would include religious thinking about human nature and the human condition as well as moral judgment and reasoning."[13]

If Gilligan's initial conclusions are sustained by further research, and Kohlberg's resolution of the apparent contradiction between their respective findings is valid, we are still left with an important question: Why do some people, particularly adult women, tend to "lead" with their faith orientation, while other adults, particularly men, speak in terms of principles of justice? However, as far as the use of the material in this book is concerned, we need not be detoured by the fact that, at least for the moment, this question remains unresolved, since:

1. The dominant stage of moral reasoning for the overwhelming majority of elementary and junior high school aged children is no higher than Stage 4. (Moral reasoning based upon principles of justice begins at Stage 5).
2. If you happen to come upon a student who has achieved a moral perspective of universal love and responsibility you can take heart from Kohlberg's contention that such a person necessarily presupposes Stage 6 principles of justice. At this point, you are free to sit back a moment and enjoy the fact that you have just met a true *tzadkanit* or *tsadik.*
3. Students who lead with their reason should be strengthened in their faith, and those who lead with their faith should be strengthened in their reason. Faith orientation and moral judgment are interlocking pieces in one's overall development as a human being, and both can and should be nourished simultaneously.

Overview and Use of This Book

Moral Development: A Practical Guide for Jewish Teachers is divided into thirteen units. Each unit contains:

1. Introduction for the Teacher
   The purpose of the teacher's introduction is to describe briefly the nature of that unit's dilemma and to suggest a procedure for presentation of the unit to the class.
2. Dilemma Story
   In most cases it has been left to the teacher to decide how the dilemma itself can best be presented. Exceptions are: Units I and II, which will be too difficult for some children to read for themselves, and should therefore be read to/with the class by the teacher, and Unit XIII, whose length and complexity demands that each student be supplied with a copy of the text. In all other cases, dilemma stories may be read to, with, or by the students.

3. Procedure and Cue Sheet

   Each unit includes a suggested procedure for its presentation. These procedures are the product of experimentation with a variety of presentational formats and are meant to help you to sequence and pace the unit. In addition, two types of supplementary discussion questions have been provided:

   a. Probe Questions

      These questions, included as a step in the suggested procedure, are meant to aid in opening up and intensifying discussion of the dilemma. Probe questions explore variations on the dilemma's main theme and raise difficulties which might otherwise be overlooked.

   b. Cue Sheets

      Following the suggested procedure for each unit, there is a short list of student comments one is likely to hear in the course of that unit's dilemma-discussion. Each of these comments is paired with a suggested teacher's response. These responses are designed to help focus discussion on possible weaknesses or contradictions in reasoning which led to the initial comment.

4. Supplementary Exercise

   The nature of these exercises varies from unit to unit. Several of the supplementary exercises involve the study of a traditional Jewish text. The exercise for Unit X, on the other hand, involves conducting a survey on a question related to that unit's dilemma. In each case, the purpose of the supplementary exercise is to provide the students with an additional opportunity to examine the issues raised in the dilemma story.

5. Additional Sources

   The supplementary materials found under the heading Additional Sources are taken primarily from either biblical or Rabbinic sources. Some, however, are of a more contemporary nature. These sources, which are included for every unit except Unit I, provide an overview of classical Jewish thinking on issues raised by the unit's dilemma. In deciding how and when to use this additional material, please keep in mind that confronting students with one of these passages *immediately* after they have done their best to resolve a dilemma through their own reasoning may prove to be counter-productive. This is especially the case if the source in question takes a position contrary to that of some of the students in the class. Premature use of a classical source may "short-circuit" a student's progress toward a rational appreciation of a particular value. It may also lead some students to conclude that the dilemma-discussion was just a cynical come-on for the subsequent dictation of traditional platitudes. To avoid this problem, it is recommended that teachers wait a few weeks after discussing the dilemma (and supplementary exercise) before using any of these sources. This interval will give students time to digest and reconsider the dilemma privately under less pressure from teacher and peers. Having allowed for this period of reflection teachers can then proceed with the important task of exposing students to the guidance of our tradition.

How you integrate a session which employs a traditional source into your ongoing lesson plans will, in some measure, depend on the nature of the source you choose to use. All traditional sources have been quoted in the original Hebrew or Aramaic to facilitate their use in a Hebrew language class. A Rabbinic epigram can be cited for both its ethical *and* its philological content. Other traditional sources have been drawn from the writings of outstanding exegetes, philosophers and halachists. Such a reference can be integrated into a history or literature lesson as an example of a given thinker's work, while at the same time serving to re-open the discussion of the dilemma which it accompanies.

A session using one of the sources might begin with a comment like, "Do you remember our discussion a few weeks ago about שם טוב? I'd like us to spend a moment looking at Rabbi Akiba's (Torah's, Rashi's, etc.) position on this issue." Since the primary function of these materials is to aid in the development of moral reasoning, a traditional source should be introduced into a revived dilemma-discussion as an *argument* or *position* which will rise or fall on its own merits, rather than a *p'sak din* which rests on the authority of its author. Respect for the sources should certainly be maintained, but not to the extent that it inhibits the source from fully "participating" in the dilemma-discussion. The give and take between source and students should be as free and critical (and respectful) as the discussion between you and the students, or between the students themselves.

Testing Procedure for Dilemmas

Though each unit's dilemma story can be approached from more than one stage of moral reasoning, the overall progression of stories has been designed to coincide roughly with the gradual widening of cognitive and social horizons which takes place during the passage to adulthood. Each unit is based on certain assumptions and styled in a way which makes it most appropriate for a particular range of ages and/or stages. Dilemmas 1-3 are designed for use in the primary grades, dilemmas 4-7 for the intermediate grades, 8-10 for the junior high grades, and dilemmas 11-13 for high school students and adults. These designations are the result of the following testing procedure:

1. Each unit was tentatively designated as most appropriate for a given grade level.
2. A rough draft of each unit was taught in a class at its assigned grade level as well as in a class one grade above and one grade below that level. These test sessions were tape recorded.
3. The tape recordings of the test sessions were reviewed to (a) determine at what age each unit appeared to induce the greatest controversy and most productive discussion, and (b) spot weaknesses in the units' structure, directions, wording, etc.
4. A second draft of each unit was prepared and retested.
5. Teachers submitted written evaluations of the revised units.
6. The written evaluations were reviewed and the indicated corrections were made.

The Talmud Torah of St. Paul, where this curriculum was tested and first employed, is both a day school (6½ hours of instruction in Jewish and secular studies *per day*) and a supplementary school (5 to 7½ hours of instruction in Jewish studies *per week*). The following was our procedure for introducing these materials into the supplementary school's curriculum.

A series of introductory seminars on the nature and purpose of cognitive-developmental moral educational was presented as part of the faculty orientation meetings held each year prior to the first week of class. At the first of these sessions, each faculty member was provided with a copy of an introduction to the materials, similar to the one you are reading now, and a brief oral presentation was made dealing with Kohlberg's research and its significance for Jewish education. In subsequent sessions teachers familiarized themselves with the definitive characteristics of the various stages in Kohlberg's taxonomy. Participants practiced fabricating comments on dilemmas (taken from the curriculum) which were typical of a given stage, and likewise, were called upon to prepare developmentally challenging responses to the comments they had fabricated. Our primary goal for these introductory seminars was to familiarize the entire faculty with the rationale, scope and methodology of the materials.

At this time it was announced that two days each year would be designated as *"Y'mei Mussar"* (Ethics Days). On these two days, one in the fall and the other in the spring, all Hebrew classes are given over to the presentation and discussion of units from this curriculum. The decision to assign the teaching of these materials to our Hebrew language teachers stemmed from our desire to avoid having the area of moral development become the special domain of "ethics teachers," or even worse, "especially ethical teachers." Making Hebrew class the setting for the presentation of the materials was also meant to signify the important position moral education occupies in the school's overall curriculum.

A few days prior to the autumn *Yom Mussar* a second series of seminars was held for teachers who actually would be presenting dilemmas to their classes later that week. At these sessions teachers were given copies of the units they would be using. In addition to reviewing the introductory information presented at the fall orientation meetings, considerable time was spent going over each teacher's assigned dilemma(s), becoming familiar with the story and supplementary sources, anticipating students' reactions, possible difficulties, etc. Teachers also viewed or listened to tape recordings of sample dilemma discussions I had held with my own classes a few days earlier. These recordings provided teachers with an opportunity to observe how students at various ages "sound" when discussing dilemmas. They also gave teachers a chance to apply what they had learned so far about how to conduct a dilemma-discussion by critiquing my performance as a discussion leader.

Following that first *Yom Mussar*, I spoke privately with each teacher who had presented a dilemma, gathering information and offering suggestions on future use of the material. I have continued this procedure with all first time dilemma-discussion teachers, and on a less formal basis with veterans. I also began to keep a written record of which classes had used which units. This was done to prevent presenting a particular dilemma to any given class more than once every 18 months or so. Our concern was that frequent repetition of a certain unit would prove to be a bit anticlimactic for many children, and that this would tend to take the creative edge off their analysis of the dilemma.

The greater flexibility in scheduling afforded by a day school format allows us to provide our day school students with quite a bit more dilemma-discussion experience. Although much of the same orientation procedure used in the supplementary school was followed with the day school faculty, the actual implementation of the materials in the day school has been quite different. Rather than structuring the presentation of dilemmas around twice yearly *Y'mei Mussar*, our day school moral development program is built on approximately 45 minutes of dilemma discussion work *per week*. This allows for much more extensive discussion of dilemmas and regular use of traditional source materials.

In our school, the planning of follow-up lessons which employ the additional sources at the end of each unit is left to the discretion of the teacher. In most cases, enough supplementary material is provided to keep a unit "afloat" for several weeks after the initial presentation of the dilemma, but we have followed no hard and fast rule in this regard. As mentioned above, our chief concern in connection with the supplementary materials is that they not be used prematurely. However, we do aim for a minimum total of two to five hours of dilemma-discussion experience per semester for each class in our afternoon school and five to eight hours per semester in our day school. These targets are based on the findings of several semester-length studies which suggest that a minimum of five to six hours of exposure to a dilemma-discussion program can significantly heighten a class' average level of moral judgment.[14]

Because these curriculum materials remain relatively new at our school, we continue to offer faculty seminars on their use each fall. At this time new faculty members can be introduced to the materials, while teachers who have had some previous experience with the curriculum can brush up on their skills and catch up on recent research developments relevant to the curriculum.

On the basis of our experience at the Talmud Torah of St. Paul, I would recommend the procedures described above as guidelines for implementation of this curriculum in your school as well.

Conclusion

The Talmud Torah of St. Paul is by no means a "home for the acutely sensitive," and yet on *Y'mei Mussar*, our hallways are filled with the sounds and gestures of moral discussion, spilling over from classrooms lit with the excitement of serious exploration of serious questions. But the waves of dialogue extend even further, as we encourage our students to continue the discussion with family and friends, retelling the dilemma, laying out their own positions on the matter, and listening to how others respond to the question. It has been my experience that moral dilemmas go where no other type of homework dares to tread, popping up in carpools, at dinner tables, in public school ... how often have I run into parents or siblings of one of my students who, having heard "the story," were anxious to tell me how *they* would solve the dilemma!

Moral development is a lifelong process. The following materials are, at best, a modest supplement to the countless opportunities for moral learning which are part and parcel of our daily lives. One might well question the need for additional, artificial dilemmas when our lives are already fraught with the actual sort. However, the materials are not intended to introduce students to the moral issues they raise so much as to provide them with a structure for the critical examination of issues with which they are familiar already; an opportunity to evaluate one's moral judgments through comparison with reasoning more and less adequate than one's own. The development of moral judgment is a dialectical process. It is my hope that you will find these materials a helpful tool for the advancement of that dialectic.

Kindergarten – 1st Grade

UNIT I – Reward and Punishment

שכר ועָנש

1. Introduction for the Teacher
2. Dilemma Story
3. Suggested Procedure and Cue Sheet
4. Supplementary Exercise
5. Drawings

About This Unit:

At the first stage of moral judgment, characteristic of early childhood, children equate what is "right" with a literal obedience to rules and authority, with avoiding punishment and not doing physical harm. In Unit I we begin the process of challenging this initial orientation. This is accomplished through exploration of a value concept which is characteristic of Stage 2 reasoning: reciprocal fairness.

Introduction for the Teacher

In his Torah commentary, Dr. Joseph Hertz notes that before eating the forbidden fruit, Adam and Eve were like children "who in the innocence and ignorance of childhood run about unclothed."[1] But Adam and Eve's unabashed nudity is not the only childlike element in their story. Their tempting of parental authority, totally ineffectual flight and awkward dissemblance are all highly evocative of the child's world. In such a setting there are a minimum number of moral categories with which one must deal: it is wrong to break a rule, disobey an authority figure or do some sort of physical damage. At this stage one's moral perspective is egocentric and literal. The recognition that ethics are essentially *social*[2] lies beyond the moral perception of a child who reasons at this level of moral judgment. The purpose of this dilemma is to draw such a child a bit closer to that perception.

The dilemma story in this unit is about two children named Ben and Batya, their father and some forbidden fruit (or to be more precise, forbidden cake). In the course of the story Ben and Batya disobey Father, making a mess of their sister's surprise birthday cake in the process. For most young children, the fact that Ben and Batya are disobedient and cause physical damage immediately identifies what they've done as "wrong," and therefore deserving of punishment. What many children will find more difficult is disassociating the moral inadmissability of what Ben and Batya do from their father's personal authority and power to punish. Such children understand obedience (as distinct from its consequences) as its own reward and are unclear about the use of non-personal standards of right and wrong (fairness, for example).[3] The exploration of these issues should form the basis of the dilemma-discussions in this unit.

In an effort to accommodate both short attention spans and jam packed lesson plans, the story has been divided into three parts. Each part ends with a dilemma question. Drawings have also been provided to supplement the dilemma.

The teacher is the best judge of how much time a class can profitably devote to discussion of the dilemma questions, though for most groups of first graders, eight to twelve minutes would be more than enough time for each question. Also, it's probably best not to cover more than two parts of the story on any single day, nor to stretch out the complete dilemma over more than a three or four day period.

Dilemma Story

Part A

Today is Jill's birthday. Father has baked her a birthday cake. It has vanilla frosting, roses and "Happy Birthday Jill" written across the top. Jill's younger brother Ben and her sister Batya ask Father if they could have a piece of cake, but Father says, "The cake's a surprise for Jill. We'll cut it at the party tonight. You'll just have to wait until then." Then Father puts the cake on the back porch so that Jill won't see it when she comes in.

Ben and Batya go out to play in the backyard. As they are playing, they see the cake and it makes them very hungry. After a while Ben says to Batya, "Maybe they'll forget to call us for dinner. Then we'll miss the party and we won't get any cake."

Batya is also worried about not getting any cake, so she says to Ben, "Let's go make sure that the cake is still safe."

Ben and Batya go over to the porch. The cake is just fine. For a long time they just stand there looking at it. Finally Ben says, "Let's just taste the frosting."

What do you think Batya should say:

"Yes, let's taste it."

or

"No, let's wait until the party."

Why?

Part B

(Finally Ben says, "Let's just taste the frosting.")

Batya says, "Well, okay, but just a *little* taste."

Batya gets a spoon and both of them take several big spoonfuls of frosting off the top of the cake. Now the cake looks very messy. Batya quickly washes the spoon and puts it back in the drawer.

Then they go out to the backyard to play some more.

When Father passes by the porch, he notices that a lot of the cake's frosting is missing and that the words "Happy Birthday Jill" are smeared. He goes outside to ask Ben and Batya if they know what happened to the cake. When Father comes close to Ben, he sees a bit of vanilla frosting on his cheek. He asks Ben, "Have you been tasting Jill's birthday cake even though I told you we'd all have to wait until the party?"

What do you think Ben should say?

Part C

Ben starts to cry. When he wipes his cheek he feels the frosting and realizes that Father knows who tasted the cake, so he says, "I tasted the frosting, but it was Batya's idea to use the spoon."

Batya says, "But it was Ben's idea to taste it."

Father replies, "I feel very badly. I'm sure Jill would have really liked the cake, but there's no time to bake or buy another one. The two of you didn't listen when I told you we'd have to wait until the party to taste the cake. Now what do you think is the fair thing to do?"

What do *you* think is the fair thing to do?

Suggested Procedure

1. Read Part A. of the dilemma story.
2. Ask the dilemma question at the end of Part A. At this point have the children respond only to *what* they think Batya should say, not *why*.
3. When every student has had an opportunity to state what they think Batya should say, go back and ask each student why they chose their particular solution. Try to alternate between students who differ as to the proper solution to the dilemma. This should help to stimulate discussion and maximize student interaction.
4. Repeat steps #1-3 above for Part B and Part C of the story. Instead of having the students simply *talk* about Part C of the dilemma, you may wish to have them *draw* their responses first. This is an excellent way to help young students think through

the problem before sharing their solutions with the rest of the class.

5. Here are some follow-up questions to stimulate discussion and direct it toward the basic issues mentioned above:

   (For the dilemma question following *Part A* of the story):

   a. If no one ever found out who tasted the frosting, would it be all right for Ben and Batya to taste it?
   b. If Father hadn't told them that they couldn't taste the cake, would it be all right for them to taste it?
   c. If the cake was for *your* birthday would you want someone to taste it before you got home? Why?

   (For the dilemma question following *Part B* of the story):

   a. If Ben lies to Father, do you think that Batya should tell on him? Why?

   (For the dilemma question following *Part C* of the story):

   a. Do you think Father should punish Ben and Batya? If "yes," why and how? (For example, should Ben and Batya be allowed to come to the birthday party?) If "no," why not?

Cue Sheet

Below, on the left, are some points your students might bring up in the course of discussing this unit's dilemma. On the right you'll find some suggested responses to these comments. These critical responses are designed to help focus discussion on possible weaknesses or contradictions in the reasoning which led to the initial comment. It is most often preferable that these sorts of responses come from other classmates, but if such challenges are not forthcoming, you yourself should provide them.

Student Statements	Possible Teacher Response
1. It would be bad taste to eat the cake.	1. Is it "bad" because of what Father said, or would it be bad even if Father had *not* told them that they's have to wait until the party to taste the cake?
2. Ben and Batya will be punished if they tell the truth.	2. But if Batya and Ben aren't honest with Father now, why should they expect Father to be honest with *them* the next time they ask *him* a question?

3. Ben and Batya shouldn't get any cake.

3. If Jill forgives them, should they get any cake?

4. Ben and Batya should say they're sorry.

4. But that won't fix the cake. Don't Ben and Batya owe Jill more than just an apology?

5. Batya and Ben should do something nice for Jill to make up for ruining her cake.

5. Give an example and explain why you think it would be a fair way to "make up."

Supplementary Exercise

A child's initial orientation toward moral problems is one of literal obedience and avoidance of punishment. The first developmental refinement in this outlook is the use of reciprocal fairness ("fair deals," or "one hand washes the other") as a standard in moral decision making.

In the following exercise, your students are given an opportunity to explore how *fairness* is a more adequate moral standard than obedience or avoidance of punishment.

Procedure:

1. Explain to the class that you'd like to talk a bit about what it is that makes a good rule "good." Tell them that you're going to give them five possible rules dealing with birthday treats in class. Slowly read the following rules to the students. During this first reading they should only *think* about which of the rules are good ones, and why.
   The rules:
   a. If you bring a treat on your birthday you must have enough for everyone in the class.
   b. If everyone's supposed to get *one* treat and someone tries to sneak *two* of them, that person shouldn't get any.
   c. If you don't *bring* treats on your birthday, you shouldn't *get* a treat on anyone else's birthday.
   d. Only those students whose birthdays fall in November should be allowed to bring treats.
   e. Treats must be something that everyone can have (no allergies, etc.).
2. Reread the rules and have the students raise their hands for each rule they think is a good one.

3. Reread the rules a third time, stopping after each one to discuss its pros and cons (follow dilemma discussion procedure, page XX, #3). In the discussion listen for students use of elements of judgment related to reciprocal fairness, i.e., "Everyone should get the same," "I should treat others like they treat me," etc. Gradually isolate these elements from the rest of the discussion, focusing in on an analysis of "fairness." What is "fairness?" How does it work? Why are "good rules" fair rules?
4. Conclude the exercise by pointing out that the sole purpose of many of the rules that teachers and parents make is to ensure that everyone is treated fairly.

Suggested Drawings for Dilemma Story

1. Today is Jill's birthday; Father has baked her a birthday cake.

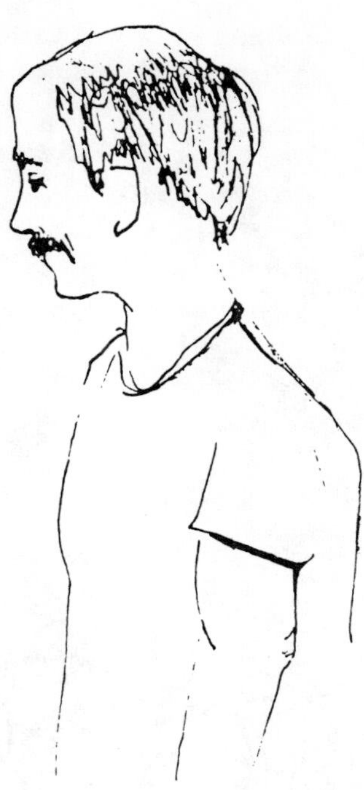

2. Ben and Batya ask Father if they could have a piece of cake . . .

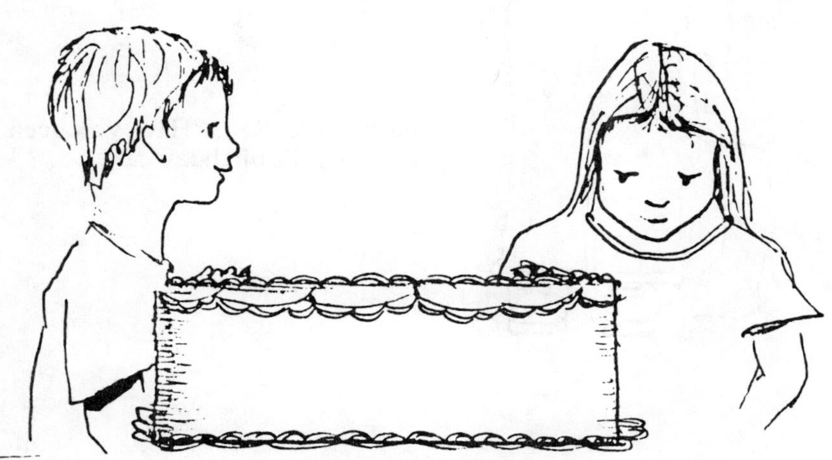

3. Finally Ben says, "Let's just taste the frosting."

4. Father asks Ben, "Have you been tasting Jill's birthday cake . . . ?"

1st Grade – 3rd Grade

UNIT II — Intentions
כונה

About This Unit

The moral distinction between intentional and unintentional acts may seem self-evident to adults, but it is a distinction that must be learned. Children reasoning at Stage 1 tend to judge actions in terms of their *physical consequences.* For such a child it may seem perfectly reasonable to conclude that someone who accidently drops a stack of dishes is more blameworthy than someone who breaks a single cup on purpose. Learning how to include *intentions* in one's moral calculations is the subject of this unit.

Introduction for the Teacher

"Your intentions are desirable but not your actions."

Sefer ha-Kuzari,
Chapter 1

The tale of the boy who blew his whistle on Yom Kippur, Peretz's story "If Not Higher," the widow's mite — what do all these stories have in common? They are identical to the extent that in each case the purpose of the story is to show that it is an act's *intent* which determines whether that act is "good." An important component of moral development for young children is a growing ability to evaluate "intent" as a distinct element in any act; without such an ability, the stories mentioned above make no sense.

The classic *halachic* sources are filled with discussions about the relationship between *what one intends to do* and *what actually happens. Kavanah* (intent), *zadon* (malicious), *sh'gagah* (accident), *p'sik resha* (an "intentional" accident) and other common Rabbinic terms signal such discussions (see Additional Sources). In the very earliest layers of *halachah,* there is already a distinction made between the legal consequences of intentional and accidental transgressions (Exodus 21:12-14; Deuteronomy 19:16-21; etc.).

In this unit we explore the relationship between the intent and results of one's actions. The unit centers around a story about a certain child who intends to do well, but is frustrated by consequences beyond her control, while another child succeeds in doing the "right thing" for the "wrong reason." The development of your student's ability to consider intent as an integral part of any moral evaluation is this unit's goal.

Dilemma Story

Kitah Alef is celebrating the first night of Chanukah. All week long Nina has been looking forward to getting a chance to light the *chanukiah*. Nina's teacher has brought her own *chanukiah* from home to use on this first night of the holiday. It is made out of clay and is very beautiful, but it is also very breakable.

All of the students would like to light the candles, but the teacher picks Nina. Nina is very excited and comes forward for the lighting. The teacher hands Nina the lighted *shamash* candle. Nina leads the class in the *brachot* and then turns to light the first candle, but in her excitement she brushes against the *chanukiah* and it falls to the floor, breaking into several pieces. Nina tries to gather up the pieces, but the teacher, who is clearly upset, asks her to be seated. Nina returns to her desk, her excitement at being chosen to light the candle is as shattered as the *chanukiah*.

After the pieces of the *chanukiah* have been cleaned up, the teacher asks for a volunteer to go to the office to get another *chanukiah*. Karen can see through the door that one of her best friends is in the hallway. Karen is not particularly interested in the party and would like to have a chance to talk to her friend about what she's planning to do after school, so she volunteers to go get a new *chanukiah*. The teacher picks Karen to get the *chanukiah*. Karen leaves the classroom to get it, stopping to talk to her friend in the hall. After talking for a couple of minutes, Karen says to her friend, "I'd rather keep on talking with you, but I'm supposed to be getting something in the office for my teacher, so I'd better go." Karen says goodbye to her friend, continues on to the office, picks up a new *chanukiah* and brings it back to her teacher. When Karen gives the teacher the *chanukiah*, the teacher says, "Thank you, Karen, for being such a good helper."

At the end of each class, Nina and Karen's teacher gives a gold star to each student who were good helpers that day. If you were the teacher, would you give Karen, or Nina, or neither, or both, a gold star for today?

Suggested Procedure

1. Read the preceding story to, or with, your students.
2. Have each student reply briefly to the question at the end of the story without yet giving reasons for their particular response.
3. After all students have had a chance to state their opinion briefly, go back and ask them to tell why they chose their solution. Try to alternate between students who differed during the initial responses as to the proper solution to the dilemma. This should help to stimulate the discussion and to challenge the students to defend or reconsider their respective positions on the issue.
4. If your students don't challenge each other with the following (or similar) questions, you may wish to ask them yourself:
   a. What does it mean when something happens "by accident?"
   b. How can you tell whether someone has done something on purpose or by accident?
   c. If two people were to hurt you, one on purpose and one by accident, who would it be easier to forgive? Why?
   d. (For those who said that Nina should *not* receive a star) If, after breaking the *chanukiah,* Nina had said, "Oh, I'm sorry! I didn't mean to break it . . ." would you have given her a star? Why?
   e. (For those who said that Karen should *not* receive a star) If Karen had wanted to get the new *chanukiah* because she also wanted to get a drink (instead of wanting to go get it in order to talk to a friend), would you give her a star? Why? What if she wanted to go because she wanted to *help* the teacher? What if she wanted to go because she wanted to *please* the teacher?
   f. (For those who said that Nina *should* receive a star because what happened was an accident) If you say that people who do something *bad* by accident shouldn't be blamed, does that also mean that people who do something *good* by accident shouldn't be rewarded? Why?

Cue Sheet

Below, on the left, are some points your students might bring up in the course of discussing this unit's dilemma. On the right you'll find some suggested responses to these comments. These critical responses are designed to help focus discussion on possible weaknesses or contradictions in the reasoning which led to the initial comment. It is most often preferable that these sorts of responses come from other classmates, but if such challenges are not forthcoming, you yourself should provide them.

Student Statements	Possible Teacher Response
1. Karen should get a star because she helped the teacher.	1. But why did she go get the *chanukiah*? She wasn't trying to help the teacher, she was trying to help herself. A *mitzvah* only counts if you really mean it.
2. Nina shouldn't get a star because she broke the teacher's *chanukiah*.	2. But you could tell she was sorry — she even tried to help pick up the pieces.
3. Both of them should get a star so that neither of them feels bad.	3. But if everyone got a star automatically, no one would do a *mitzvah* in order to get one (as a reward).
4. Karen shouldn't get a star because she stopped to talk with her friend.	4. What's wrong with helping yourself at the same time you're helping someone else?
5. Neither of them should get a star because both of them did something bad.	5. But what Nina *wanted* to do was right; she did the wrong thing by accident. What Karen *wanted* to do was wrong — she kind of did the *right* thing by accident.

Supplementary Exercise

The objectives of the following exercise are:

1. To give the students some practice analyzing *intentions*.
2. To introduce the students to the value terms *chayav* (obligated to pay) and *patur* (not obligated to pay).

A suggested procedure is as follows:

Explain to the students that you are going to tell them three very short stories about how someone's property came to be damaged, and that after each story you're going to ask them who they think is *chayav* (and who *patur*). After they have fully discussed each case, tell the class which one Maimonides (the Rabbi who wrote the stories) considered *chayav* and why.

1. Two people are passing through a public place. One of them is running and one of them is walking. They accidentally bump into one another causing some sort of damage. Who is *chayav* and who is *patur*? Why? (Maimonides declares the person who is running *chayav* because his behavior is "unconventional.")
2. Two people are passing through a public place. One of them is running and one of them is walking. They accidentally bump into one another, causing some sort of damage. It is just about time for Shabbat to begin. Who is *chavav* and who is *patur*? Why? (Maimonides declares the person who is running *patur*. He assumes that the runner is making inavoidable last minute preparations for Shabbat. Is this a reasonable assumption in your community? Consider other assumptions of this sort.)
3. A person is climbing a ladder. One of the ladder's rungs breaks off and damages something down below. If the ladder was unstable and weak, is the climber *chayav* or *patur*? If the ladder was strong and stable, or at least appeared to be stable, is the climber *chayav* or *patur*? (Maimonides declares that if the ladder was weak and unstable the climber is *chayav*, but if the ladder was strong, or at least appeared to be so, the climber is *patur*. Damage resulting from carelessness cannot be considered purely accidental. The party who causes the damage is therefore *chayav*).

Mishneh Torah, Hilchot Hovel 6:4, 9

Additional Sources

For a description of additional sources and suggestions for their use, see the Introduction, pp. 26-27.

From Rabbinic Literature

1. *Mitzvot* must be intentional.

Berachot 13

1. מצוות צריכות כוונה (ברכות י״ג).

2. *Mitzvot* needn't be intentional.

Rosh Ha-Shanah 28

2. מצוות אין צריכות כוונה (ראש ה׳, כ״ח)

3. R. Nahman, the son of Yizhak, said: A sin performed with good intention is better than a *mitzvah* done with evil intention. But

hasn't R. Yehudah, citing Rav, said: People should continue with Torah and *mitzvot*, even if it be for some ulterior motive, for eventually they may come to do them without ulterior motives? Okay, then: (a sin done with good intention is) *as good* as a *mitzvah* performed for an ulterior motive.

Nazir 23

3. אמר ר׳ נחמן בר יצחק: גדולה עבירה לשמה ממצווה שלא לשמה. והאמר רב יהודה אמר רב: לעולם יעסוק אדם בתורה ובמצוות אפילו שלא לשמן שמתוך שלא לשמן בא לשמן. אלא אימא כמצווה שלא לשמה (נזיר כ״ג)

4. Though one may do much and another just a little, the important thing is that it is done out of devotion to God.

Berachot 5

4. אחד המרבה ואחד הממעיט ובלבד שיכוון את ליבו לשמים (ברכות, ה׳).

5. The Holy One Who is Blessed requires the (devotion of one's) heart, as it is said: "But the Lord looks to the heart" (I Samuel 16:7).

Sanhedrin, 106

5. הקדוש ברוך הוא לבא בעי, שנאמר: והי׳ יראה ללבב (סנה׳ קי״ו).

6. If someone is walking by a synagogue, or their house is located next to a synagogue, and they happen to hear a shofar or the reading of the *megillah* and they concentrate (on the sound), they therefore fulfill the *mitzvah*, and if they don't (concentrate) they haven't fulfilled the *mitzvah*.

Rosh Ha-Shanah 56

6. היה עובר אחורי בית הכנסת או שהיה ביתו סמוך לבית הכנסת ושמע קול שופר או קול מגילה אם כוון לבו יצא ואם לאו לא יצא (ראש ה׳, נ״ו).

2nd Grade – 4th Grade

UNIT III — A Good Name

שם טוב

1. Introduction for the Teacher
2. Dilemma Story
3. Suggested Procedure and Cue Sheet
4. Supplementary Exercise
5. Additional Sources

About This Unit

At the first two stages of moral reasoning, children tend to justify doing what they perceive as right on the basis of that right action's direct material consequences. Beginning at Stage 3, however, certain indirect consequences of one's actions come to play a major role in moral decision making. It is at this stage that *expectations* associated with well-defined relationships become an important moral standard: what is right is to live up to such expectations — to be a good sister, son, friend, etc.

This unit deals with roles and expectations and, as such, is particularly appropriate for children who reason at Stage 2 or 3.

Introduction For the Teacher

Early on in most children's moral development comes the recognition that the community sets standards of behavior by which we evaluate others and are evaluated ourselves. You and I might agree that a certain individual is a "good person" because we share a common definition of what makes a person "good." When most of the people of a given community agree upon such a definition, it becomes a community standard. A child's recognition of this process leads to the understanding that how one is *treated* by others is closely related to how one is *perceived* vis-a-vis these standards.

But this process of evaluation is not simply a matter of measuring each action in turn, as if an action stands alone — isolated and unrelated to actions which come before or after. Rather, we seek out patterns in these measured perceptions and form *images* of one another from these patterns. One's image is a significant factor in evaluating a given action and is in turn itself re-evaluated in the light of that action. For example: A store owner notices a certain child wandering aimlessly through the store. The owner has caught this child shoplifting on several previous occasions. The *image* of the child as a shoplifter influences how the owner perceives the child's present behavior. The owner decides to watch the child closely, not simply on the basis of the child's aimless wandering but, rather, as a consequence of the child's present wandering in conjunction with his or her previously established image. Furthermore, what the child does on this occasion will influence the owner's subsequent image of the child.

There is a traditional Jewish term for someone who has established an image of personal integrity, consistently meeting or exceeding the community's ethical standards. The Bible and Rabbinic literature describe such a person as having acquired a *shem tov*, a "good name" (see Additional Sources for references). This unit is intended to help children understand how a good name is acquired and retained, and to appreciate its value.

The focal point of the unit is the dilemma story. The Supplementary Exercise and Additional Sources are included as resources and may be used as desired. However, when at least one of the biblical or Rabbinic sources cited is used, the students are exposed to an example of traditional Jewish literature, as well as becoming familiar with the Hebrew term *shem tov*.

The class must analyze and seek the best resolution to the dilemma presented by the story. In the course of the discussion, it is useful to take the following points into consideration. If the students don't raise these points on their own, you may want to guide the discussion toward their consideration:

1. People usually rely on generalized perceptions (images) in the formation of interpersonal relationships.
2. The essence of one's name (*shem*) is consistency: a *shem* is a generalization, an evaluated image. One's every action tends to be evaluated in the context of one's previously established *shem*.
3. A *shem tov* strengthens and enriches one's relationships with others by establishing a foundation of trust and a reservoir of good will which may help to sustain relationships during occasional moments of "bad faith."

Dilemma Story

Part A

Kitah Bet collected *tzedakah*.

It was the job of the treasurer to take the *tzedakah* home each weekend, count it and report back to the class the next week. Sandy was elected treasurer at the beginning of the year.

On a certain weekend Sandy's family was going out of town, so a substitute treasurer needed to be appointed. Sandy suggested that David be her substitute, but Becky claimed that David should not be allowed to substitute because last year he did not turn in all the *Keren Ami* money he'd collected, and several class members agreed.

Becky said: "Everybody likes you David, but we should pick someone we can trust."

David responded: "How can you say you like me if you don't let me be treasurer?! This time is different. Give me a chance. I promise that the money will be safe with me."

The class felt that Sandy should decide whether David could be the treasurer. Sandy was reluctant to be the one to make the choice, especially since she had been in a different class last year and this was the first she'd heard about David and the missing *Keren Ami* money. Nevertheless, the class insisted that she make the decision, so she did.

Part B

Sandy decided to choose David as her substitute. But just to be on the safe side, she counted the money before handing it over to David. David was very proud of having been made treasurer. When he got home he showed his mother the *tzedakah* box. His mother said that she was very proud of him, too, and she reminded him of how important it was for him to take good care of the money.

On Sunday morning David's older brother came into David's room to borrow some money from him for a movie he wanted to see that afternoon. David was still sleeping. His brother saw the box of money on David's dresser. Thinking that the money belonged to David and that David wouldn't mind if he borrowed some of it, he helped himself to three dollars from the box.

When David's brother got back from the movie, he told David that he had taken the money and that he'd pay him back as soon as he could.

David was very upset. He explained to his brother that the money he had taken was *tzedakah* and that he needed it back right away. But David's brother replied, "What's the big deal, anyway? I'll pay you back when I get my allowance. You'll just have to wait a few days, that's all."

David spent much of Sunday afternoon thinking over what he should do. He came up with three ideas:

1. Borrow three dollars from his mother, put it in the box and not tell anyone what had happened. But David was reluctant to do

this because it would be difficult to explain to his mother why he needed the money. He also didn't want to get his brother in trouble for taking it.
2. Return the box without replacing the three dollars and hope that no one would notice the missing money.
3. Return the box without replacing the three dollars, explain what had happened to the class, and hope they'd understand.

Which of these three ideas do you think is the best way for David to deal with his problem? Why?

Suggested Procedure

1. Introducing the dilemma:
   Ask the students for a definition of "treasurer." Then ask: What do you need (what attributes are needed) to be a good treasurer? Most likely a mix of intellectual, ethical and even physical attributes will be suggested. Offer the dilemma story as a way of sorting out these attributes.
2. Visual Aids:
   If desired, display cards with the characters' names and some short identifying phrase (e.g., Sandy: permanent treasurer; David's brother: owes $3.00 to *tzedakah*, etc.) as a way of helping the students to keep the various characters straight during the discussion. Be careful to keep the identifying phrase non-judgmental.
3. Before going on to Part B, discuss the following questions with the class:
   a. What points should Sandy consider which are in David's favor? What considerations might go against making David the substitute treasurer?
      When a list of "points for consideration" (by Sandy) has been developed, discussion should be directed toward analyzing how these pros and cons relate to David's *shem* (image, reputation).
   b. What is it (what does David have) which makes the class reluctant to make David treasurer? (A *Shem Ra*: "a bad name" — teach the term.)

Cue Sheet

Below on the left, are some points your students might bring up in the course of discussing this unit's dilemma. On the right you'll find some suggested responses to these comments. These critical responses are designed to help focus discussion on possible weaknesses or contradictions in the reasoning which led to the initial comment. It is most often preferable that these sorts of responses come from other classmates, but if such challenges are not forthcoming, you yourself should provide them.

Student Statements	Possible Teacher Response
1. David should tell his mother what happened and borrow the money from her.	1. Assuming his mother lent him the money, do you think David is still obligated to tell the class what happened?
2. David should return the box and not say anything. If he tells them what happened, they probably won't believe him anyway, and he can still secretly put the money back when his brother repays him.	2. Do you mean that if a person thinks that he or she won't be believed when telling the truth, that they might as well do or say whatever is in their own best interest? Should you only tell the truth if it gets you what you want?
3. David did the best he could — he didn't mean to lose the money, it was an accident. He should just tell the class what happened. If the other kids are worth having as friends, they'll forgive him.	3. David had a responsibility to the group. If Sandy had been as careless as David, there would have been no *tzedakah* left by this time. The class has every right not to let David ever be treasurer again.
4. He should tell his mother what has happened. It's his brother's own fault if his brother gets in trouble.	4. It's true that David lost the money by accident, but it's also true that his brother took the money by accident, so if there's a punishment, they should share it.
5. David's brother didn't seem to care much about David. I don't see why David should try to protect him.	5. Doesn't David have a responsibility to be loyal to his brother? If he was in his brother's place, wouldn't he want his brother to be loyal to him?

Supplementary Exercise

Popularity and Shem Tov

We call people popular if many others enjoy being with them. A popular person is "well liked."

Does having a *shem tov* automatically make one popular? Do popular people always have a *shem tov*? This exercise is meant to help the students distinguish ethical characteristics (which contribute to the acquisition of a *shem tov*) from other personal traits which might also be considered desirable.

Here's a list of characteristics which could describe someone who is popular. Distribute this list to the students and ask each of them to check off those characteristics which specifically contribute to the acquisition of a *shem tov*.

cute	trustworthy
honest	brave
humorous	athletic
gets good grades	smart
talented	nice dresser
fair	rich

Have the students compare and discuss their lists. Consider the question: What makes a trait relevant to *shem tov*? Now discuss the following: Does it matter which ones were checked off? Could a person have the checked off some of the characteristics but not the others, or all the others but none of the ones that they originally checked off? Or could they have checked every characteristic? How does the image of a person change as the characteristics ascribed to him or her change? (This lesson could be done in Hebrew and thus double as a review of adjectives.)

Additional Sources

Biblical Sources

1. Wisdom begins with the fear of the Lord; All who do (God's will) are well respected, their praise will long endure.

Psalms 111:10

1. ראשית חכמה יראת ה״; שכל טוב לכל עשיהם, תהילתו עומדת לעד (תהלים קיא:י).

2. A good name is preferable to great riches, favor is better than silver and gold.

Proverbs 22:1

2. נבחר שם מעשר רב, מכסף ומזהב חן טוב (משלי כב:א).

3. So shall you find favor and respect in the sight of God and humanity.

Proverbs 3:4

3. ומצא חן ושכל טוב בעיני אלוהים ואדם (משלי ג:ד).

4. A (good) name is better than fine perfume.

Ecclesiastes 7:1

4. טוב שם משמן טוב (קהלת ז:א).

5. ... they would stigmatize me by giving me a bad name....

Nehemiah 6:13

5. והיה להם לשם רע למען יחרפוני (נחמיה ו:יג).

Rabbinic and Halachic Sources

1. Those who acquire a good name, acquire it for themselves; those who acquire Torah acquire the world to come.

Avot 2:8

1. קנה שם טוב קנה לעצמו; קנה לו דברי תורה קנה לו חיי העולם הבא (אבות ב:ח).

2. Rabbi Simeon says: "There are three crowns, the crown of the Torah, the crown of the priesthood and the crown of royalty. But greater than all of these is the crown of a good name.

Avot 4:17

2. רבי שמעון אומר: שלשה כתרים הן: כתר תורה, וכתר כהונה, וכתר מלכות. וכתר שם טוב עולה על גביהן (אבות ד:יז).

3. The person who is designated to withdraw funds from the Temple treasury does not enter the room where the funds are kept when he is wearing a cloak with a folded border, or shoes, or sandals, or *tefillin*, or an amulet, lest he become poor and people say that his poverty resulted from a sin he committed in the room where the funds are kept — (i.e., punishment for stealing from the treasury and hiding the money in his clothing). Likewise, lest he become rich and people say he embezzled funds from the Temple treasury. For it is a person's duty to be free of blame before human beings as before God, as it is said (Numbers 32): "And be guiltless before the Lord and before Israel," and

again it says: "And so shall you find favor and good repute in the sight of God and human beings."

Shekalim 3:2

(Explanatory note: This passage from the *Mishnah* means that treasurers for the *Bet Ha-Mikdash* were not allowed to wear clothing in which money could be hidden while they were in the treasury room because, according to this *halachah*, not only must we *be* honest, but we must also *appear* to be honest. We should conduct ourselves in a way that avoids making others suspicious of us.)

3. אין התורם נכנס לא בפרגוד חפות ולא במנעל ולא בסנדל ולא בתפילין ולא בקמיע, שמא יעני ויאמרו מעון הלשכה העני; או שמא יעשיר ויאמרו מתרומת הלשכה העשיר. לפי שאדם צריך לצאת ידי המקום שנאמר: והייתם נקיים מה׳ ומישראל (במדבר לב), ואומר: ומצא חן ושכל טוב בעיני אלוהים ואדם. (שקלים ג:ב).

4. Whenever people spend their time doing *mitzvot* they are acquiring for themselves a good name. You find that a person is called by three names: One is what their mother and father call them, another is what other people call them, and a third is what they acquire for themselves.

They said to Solomon: What do you mean by "A good name is better than fine perfume?" He said to them: When a person is born, no one knows who he or she is. If they die with a good name they leave behind good deeds, the community attends to their (burial) needs and they declare their praise, saying: so and so how much *tzedakah* he gave! How much Torah he learned! How many *mitzvot* he did! May he therefore rest with the righteous ....

Midrash Tanhuma, VaYachel

4. כל זמן שאדם מרבה במצוות קונה שייט לעצמו. את מוצא שלשה שמות נקראו לו לאדם: אחד מה שקוראים לו אביו ואמו ואחד מה שקוראין לו בני אדם. ואחד מה שקונה הוא לעצמו טוב מכולן מה שקונה הוא לעצמו.

אמרו לשלמה: מה ״טוב שם משמן טוב״? אמר להם: בשעה שאדם נולד אין הכל יודעים מי הוא. נפטר בשם טוב משפיע מעשים טובים באין ישראל מטפלין עמו, עושים עמו גמילות חסר, מכריזין שבחו ואומרים ״פלוני זה כמה צדקות, כמה תורה, כמה מצוות עשה, משכבו תהא עם צדיקים. (תנחי , פי ויקהל).

5. "A good name is better than fine perfume." Fine perfume flows downward while a good name ascends. Fine perfume is transient while a good name endures forever. Fine perfume can be used up, but a good name is not used up. Fine perfume is bought with money, while a good name is free. Fine perfume is for the living while a good name is for the living and the dead. Fine perfume can only be acquired by the rich, while a good name can be acquired by rich and poor. Fine perfume is diffused from the bedroom to the dining room, while a good name is diffused throughout the world. Fine perfume on a corpse becomes rancid, while a good name on a corpse does not become rancid. Fine perfume falls upon water and is washed away, while a good name falls upon water and is not washed away. Fine perfume burns up when it falls into a fire, while a good name is not burned up when it falls into a fire.

R. Judah b. R. Simon said: We find men who had been anointed with fine oils entered the place of life and came out burned, while men of good name entered the place of death and came out alive. Nadav and Abihu entered the place of life and died. Hananiah, Michael, and Azariah entered a terrible furnace and came out alive. That's why it says: "A good name is better than fine perfume."

5. ״טוב שם משמן טוב״: שמן טוב יורד ושם טוב עולה; שמן טוב לשעתו ושם טוב לעולם; שמן טוב כלה ושם טוב אינו כלה; שמן טוב בדמים ושם טוב בחינם; שמן טוב נוהג בחיים ושם טוב נוהג בחיים ובמתים; שמן טוב בעשירים ושם טוב בעניים ובעשירים; שמן טוב הולך מקיטון לטרקלין ושם טוב הולך מסוף העולם ועד סופו; שמן טוב נופל על המת ומבאיש... שם טוב נופל על מתים ואינו מבאיש... שמן טוב נופל על המים ונידוח ושם טוב נופל על המים ואינו נידוח.... שמן טוב נופל על האור ונשרף ושם טוב נופל על האור ואינו נשרף.

אמר ר׳ יהודה בר סימון: מצינו בעלי שמן טוב נכנסו למקום חיים ויצאו הם שרופין, ובעלי שם טוב נכנסו למקום מתים ויצאו חיים: נדב ואביהוא נכנסו למקום חיים ומתו. חנניה, מישאל ועזריה נכנסו לאתון נורא ויצאו חיים; לכך נאמר: טוב שם משמן טוב.... (קהלת רבה, ז׳).

6. *Shulchan Aruch*: Be careful not to call someone by a nickname which suggests something bad (*shem ra*) about him or her, even if

that person is used to it. If the intent is to embarrass that person it is forbidden.

Hoshen Mishpat 228:5

6. יזהר שלא לכנות שם רע לחברו אע״פ שהוא רגיל באותו כינוי; אם כוונתו לביישו אסור (חושן משפט רכח:ה׳).

3rd Grade – 5th Grade

UNIT IV — Rights and Privileges

זכויות

1. Introduction for the Teacher
2. Dilemma Story
3. Procedure and Cue Sheet
4. Supplementary Exercise
5. Additional Sources

About This Unit

To children who reason at Stage 2, *fairness* means giving all concerned an equal share of whatever there is to divide. There is certainly something to be said for this quantitative understanding of fairness, but it is not without its inadequacies as a standard of justice. Exploring those inadequacies is the subject of this unit.

Introduction for the Teacher

We invest considerable time and effort in teaching children that following equitable rules makes for "fair play," preventing favoritism and thus greatly facilitating any cooperative effort. It should therefore come as no great surprise that children often conclude that "fairness" is the ultimate moral value.

However, if by fairness one means a simple, unbending egalitarianism, is this standard, in fact, an adequate moral arbiter for any dilemma? Or is there such a thing as a morally dictated exception to the rule? The premise of the following unit is that in some situations, facile fairness comes up short.

The challenge to fairness can come from two sides. A *less* mature value structure can resist fairness out of simple self-interest. This unit is intended for children who have, at least intellectually, concluded that fairness is superior to unchecked selfishness as a moral standard. But fairness can also be challenged from a *more* mature value structure and this is the challenge upon which this unit is built.

The challenge implicit in this dilemma-discussion comes from the idea of human rights. Rights can be seen as *a priori* privileges, privileges which precede any fairness generating system. If a system fairly satisfies the rights of most, but not all, of its constituents, what should bend: the absolute fairness of the system or the unmet rights of the individual? This is the issue at stake in the following dilemma story. What should one do when an individual's request for special treatment, a request based upon that individual's recognized rights, collides with the need for equity within the group?

Dilemma Story

Camp Tzedek is run on a budget. This means that each year a certain amount of money is available for operating the camp. Camp Tzedek can spend only as much money as is in the budget.

Each winter the Board of Directors of the camp meets to decide on a budget for the coming summer. One winter the Board finds that it will be able to meet all expected costs for the coming camp season and still have a considerable amount of money left over. The Board comes up with the idea of polling those children who will be attending the camp that summer to determine what they would most like to see done with the extra money.

The Board of Directors decides that (*whatever the class has chosen*) is a worthwhile use of the extra money, and directs the appropriate committee to go ahead with its use for that purpose.

During the first week of May, Susan signs up to attend Camp Tzedek. Susan's legs are paralyzed and she can only get around by using a wheelchair. She's a proud child who likes to do things for herself, but this sometimes requires special equipment: ramps or elevators instead of steps, support railings in the bathroom, a desk that can fit her wheelchair, etc. Up until this year Susan had gone with her family to their lake cabin each summer, but she now wants to attend Camp Tzedek with other children she knows.

At its summer meeting, the Board of Directors is informed of Susan's application. The question is raised as to how the camp could pay for special equipment for Susan, seeing as all the coming year's funds had already been budgeted. At this point the Board member who was overseeing the "extra money" for (*whatever the class has chosen*) states that it had not yet been spent and was still in the bank. Perhaps this money could be used to make the necessary changes for Susan. Another Board member responds: "But is it right to deprive all the other children of something which is valuable to the camp for the benefit of one child?" The Board decides to poll the children again.

Here's the question they asked:

A child who has applied to Camp Tzedek is confined to a wheelchair. If she is to attend camp, several items must be purchased to meet her special needs. It has been suggested that the money which you had decided should go for __________ could be used to make these purchases. Do you think this money should be used for this new purpose?

Suggested Procedure

1. Read the first two paragraphs of the dilemma story to the class. At this point solicit a few suggestions from the class as to what they would want done for the camp with surplus funds. Have the class choose the suggestion they like best. The class' choice can then stand for the result of the "poll."
2. Read the rest of the dilemma. Poll the class on the concluding question. Discuss their respective positions on the issue. Re-poll the class at the end of the period to see if anyone's position has changed, and if so, why.
3. Interject the following "what ifs" into the discussion:
   a. What if Susan's parents could themselves pay for the necessary adaptations, but are not willing to do so?
   b. What if no other children (unless they were also confined to a wheelchair) would be allowed to use Susan's special equipment (the elevator, for example)?

Cue Sheet

Below, on the left, are some points your students might bring up in the course of discussing this unit's dilemma. On the right you'll find some suggested responses to these comments. These critical responses are designed to help focus discussion on possible weaknesses or contradictions in the reasoning which led to the initial comment. It is most often preferable that these sorts of responses come from other classmates, but if such challenges are not forthcoming, you yourself should provide them.

Student Statements	Possible Teacher Response
1. It's not fair for Susan to get special treatment. If the changes are made for Susan, only *one person* benefits; the other way, *lots of people* benefit.	1. What if Susan were your sister?

2. Why doesn't Susan go to a camp especially for handicapped children?

2. If such a camp were further away than camp Tzedek, would you be willing to help pay for her added travel expenses?

3. If Susan's parents can afford to pay an extra fee, camp is not obligated to make the necessary changes. Her parents should at least *offer* to help pay for Susan's equipment.

3. People who aren't handicapped are obligated to help those who are. I'd feel bad about it if Susan couldn't come to camp. If her parents won't do their fair share, everyone else should pitch in a little more.

4. It would be mean not to let Susan attend the camp.

4. If the other campers aren't prepared to accept Susan, it could end up being a miserable summer for *everyone*.

5. They should do whatever the result of the second poll says to do. The majority rules.

5. Don't people have certain rights, whether or not the majority recognizes them?

Supplementary Exercise

The following story is taken from the *Talmud* (*Yoma* 35b). It records an incident in the life of Hillel the Elder (60 B.C.E. – 10 C.E.). Some children may see what Hillel does in this story as dishonest, or unfair to the "paying students." A discussion of the appropriateness of Hillel's actions can serve as a review of concepts and issues which were raised in this unit's main dilemma story.

Hillel the Elder spent part of each day doing physical labor, for which he received a daily wage. Half of his wages he would give to the doorkeeper of the school he attended as a fee for that day's class, and with the other half he supported his family.

One day, in the month Tevet, Hillel could find no work. Since he could not pay the doorkeeper the daily entrance fee, he was not allowed to enter the classroom. Hillel did not want to miss that day's lesson, so he climbed up on the school's roof and listened to the lesson through the skylight. While he was listening, a heavy snow began to fall.

After a while one of the teachers in the classroom noticed that the room had become quite dark. He looked up and saw someone on the skylight. The class climbed up on the roof and found Hillel lying there, covered by a layer of snow. They removed the now shivering Hillel and brought him inside to warm up by the fire.

Question: Was anyone in this story treated unfairly? Who? Why?

אמרו עליו על הלל הזקן שבכל יום ויום היה עושה ומשתכר בטרפעיק. חציו היה נותן לשומר בית המדרש וחציו לפרנסתו ולפרנסת אנשי ביתו. פעם אחת לא מצא להשתכר ולא הניחו שומר בית המדרש לכנס. עלה ונתלה וישב על פי ארבה, כדי שישמע דברי אלהים חיים מפי שמעיה ואבטליון. אמרו: אותו היום ערב שבת היה ותקופת טבת היתה, וירד עליו שלג מן השמים (וכסהו). כשעלה עמוד השחר אמר לו שמעיה לאבטליון: אבטליון אחי, בכל יום הבית מאיר והיום אפל, שמא יום מענן הוא? הציצו עיניהם וראו דמות אדם בארבה. עלו ומצאו עליו רום שלוש אמות שלג. פרקוהו והרחיצוהו וסכוהו והושיבוהו כנגד המדורה.

Additional Sources

This newspaper article describes a court case which is similar in many ways to this unit's dilemma story. You may wish to share this article with your class.

COURT TO HEAR SCHOOL APPEAL ON HANDICAPS LAW

Washington, April 30 — The U.S. Supreme Court agreed Monday to hear a university's appeal from a court order that it provide a sign-language "interpreter" for a deaf graduate student.

The case gives the high court an opportunity to define the scope of the law that prohibits discrimination against the handicapped by institutions that receive federal funds. In the years since Congress passed that law, Rehabilitation Act of 1973, the handicapped have become increasingly willing to assert their legal rights, and public debate on the issue has grown.

Section 504 of the law provides that no "otherwise qualified" handicapped person shall "be excluded from participation in, be denied the benefits of, or be subjected to discrimination under" federally aided programs.

That section was invoked by Walter Camenisch, a master's degree candidate at the University of Texas, who argued that he needed instruction in sign language to benefit from the program.

A federal district court agreed, issuing a preliminary injunction and ordering the university to provide an interpreter until a full trial could be held. The U.S. Court of Appeals for the Fifth Circuit affirmed the injunction.

No trial has been held, and Camenisch has since graduated. However, he still has a financial stake in the case because the district court required him to post a $3,000 bond with which to reimburse the university if he lost the case.

In its appeal, the university argues that while Section 504 prohibits discrimination, it was not intended by Congress to impose financial obligations on the recipients of federal funds. The university also argues that the section permits lawsuits only by the federal government, not individuals.

If justices decide that the law did not give Camenisch the right to sue, it will not reach the broader issue of how far the university's obligation extends.

The justices considered Section 504 once before, in a 1979 case involving a deaf woman who sought admission to a graduate nursing program. The justices ruled unanimously that the woman's rejection did not violate Section 504 because, due to her deafness, she was not "otherwise qualified" to be a registered nurse.

In the case accepted yesterday, both sides agreed that Camenisch's handicap did not disqualify him from an administrative job at a school for the deaf, the job for which he was seeking graduate training.

4th Grade – 7th Grade

UNIT V — Gossip or Slander

לשון הרע

1. Introduction for the Teacher
2. Dilemma Story
3. Suggested Procedure and Cue Sheet
4. Supplementary Exercise
5. Additional Sources

About This Unit

When I was a child my mother would often tell me, "If you can't say something nice about someone don't say anything at all." I recently visited a friend's home where a crocheted pillow case proclaimed, "If you can't say anything nice about someone sit by me."

What is the moral status of gossip? Is it always undesirable to speak negatively about others? Can such talk ever serve a worthwhile purpose? These are some of the questions raised by this unit's dilemma.

For Stage 2 thinkers, the question of whether or not it is right to relate a particular piece of negative information about someone to a third party will be resolved on the basis of one's personal relationship with those two parties ("He wouldn't talk that way about me, so I won't talk that way about him"). Stage 3 thinkers will emphasize the formal expectations and obligations which are a part of personal relationships ("Nice people don't gossip"; "Friends don't gossip about one another"). Stage 4 thinkers will show concern for the social consequences of gossip ("For the good of the group, everyone should know exactly what happened").

Introduction for the Teacher

Halachah distinguishes between actions which are forbidden under normal circumstances and actions which are forbidden in a more absolute sense. For instance, certain activities which are normally forbidden on Shabbat are allowed, if necessary to save a life (*pekuach nefesh*). On the other hand, *halachah* absolutely forbids committing murder, incest or idolatry, even at the threat of one's own life (*Sanhedrin* 74a). The Tannaim who framed this *halachah* considered these three acts to be radically incompatible with Torah.

In numerous subsequent Talmudic dicta, a fourth transgression is added to these three arch sins: *lashon hara*: an evil tongue. In these same sources it is even maintained that *lashon hara* can be, both figuratively and literally, a type of murder (*J. Peah* 1:1, *Yoma* 9; *Arachin* 15). We may conclude from this treatment in the classical Rabbinic sources that the Rabbis considered it among the most reprehensible of human activities.

What, exactly, is *lashon hara*, and how does it operate? Maimonides defines *lashon hara* as speaking disparagingly of others "even if it's the truth."[1] It is alternately translated as gossip, talebearing, slander or scandal mongering.

The motivation for engaging in *lashon hara* is complex. It can be used to cement intra-group relationships, relieve feelings of inferiority or jealousy, harm rivals or impress friends. But perhaps its most dangerous characteristic is that it can be engaged in under the most casual of circumstances. Since it usually has the guise of being socially ingratiating and acceptable, it often appears to be harmless. Thus, the temptation to accept and pass along *lashon hara* is often difficult to resist.

In this unit's dilemma story, two friends are confronted with a perfect opportunity for *lashon hara*. Whether this casual conversation between friends should include "speaking disparagingly of others even if it's the truth" is the dilemma your students must ponder.

Dilemma Story

Miriam and Carla stole a box of candy from their teacher's desk. The teacher kept the candy as an occasional treat for the class. Miriam and Carla were caught and agreed to pay for the candy.

The next day the principal asked Miriam and Carla's teacher to discuss the problem of stealing with her class. So, that afternoon the teacher set aside the time usually spent on math for the discussion. The teacher began by saying that the fact that they were having the discussion instead of the regular math lesson showed how important she felt it was for the students to discuss the issue. The teacher then went on to explain about the stolen candy, though she didn't mention that it was Carla and Miriam who had taken it. Even so, Richard, one of the students in the class, had the strong feeling that everyone except for himself knew who had stolen the candy.

After class, Richard, you and another friend are walking home together. Richard says, "I had the feeling in class today that everyone knew who had stolen the candy but me."

Your friend replies, "I think I know who stole it."

"You do?" asks Richard. "Will you tell me?"

Your friend turns to you and says, "Well, everyone else already knows anyway. Let's tell him."

What should you say?

a. Richard's our friend. Let's tell him.
b. The teacher said that it's important for us to discuss it. Let's tell him.
c. No. Don't tell him.

Suggested Procedure

1. Read the story to, or with, the class.
2. Ask each student to state which solution to the dilemma (a, b or c) they prefer.
3. Ask for individuals to explain or defend the solution they have chosen, alternating between students who differ as to which solution is preferable. You may wish to use the following questions and comments to stimulate discussion, point out weak or contradictory reasoning, etc.:
   a. Would your opinion change if Miriam or Carla were your best friend? Why?
   b. Would your opinion change if Richard was your best friend? Why?
   c. Does it make any difference whether your friend really did know who stole the candy, or merely thought he knew who stole it, in deciding whether or not he, in turn, should tell Richard? Why?
   d. Which solution would you prefer if you were Miriam or Carla? Why?
   e. In terms of right or wrong, does it make any difference whether you are *telling* about or *listening* to unflattering information about others?
4. Re-poll the students as to which solution they now prefer.
5. (Optional) In a subsequent class session, do the supplementary exercise on *lashon hara* and the news. It might be best not to do the supplementary exercise during the same week as the presentation of the dilemma. In this way, students whose views on the dilemma story were at wide variance with the guidelines on *lashon hara* set down by Rambam will not feel totally squelched or betrayed in return for their candidness.

Cue Sheet

Below, on the left, are some points your students might bring up in the course of discussing this unit's dilemma. On the right you'll find some suggested responses to these comments. These critical responses are designed to help focus discussion on possible weaknesses or contradictions in the reasoning which led to the initial comment. It is most often preferable that these sorts of responses come from other classmates, but if such challenges are not forthcoming, you yourself should provide them.

Student Statements	Possible Teacher Responses
1. It all depends on who were my closer friends: Miriam and Carla, or Richard.	1. But if all three of them were equally good friends, how would you decide?
2. Gossip makes people real paranoid and distrustful.	2. Don't people have the right to know who they should be careful about — who they shouldn't trust?
3. There's no reason to further embarrass Miriam and Carla. I wouldn't want everyone talking about me like that.	3. But maybe the embarrassment they would suffer would discourage others from doing what they did.
4. It's fun and interesting to know who did what.	4. Is entertaining oneself a good enough reason to ruin someone else's reputation?
5. I'd want my friend to tell *me* if *I* didn't know, so it's only fair that I tell him/her.	5. Why do you think the teacher didn't mention any names during the class discussion?

Supplementary Exercise

1. In this section you will find a selection from Maimonides' *Mishneh Torah* on *rechilut* (gossip) and *lashon hara* (slander). Go over this selection with your class so that each student clearly understands Maimonides' definition of *rechilut* and *lashon hara*. If you plan to study this passage in the original Hebrew, you may need to spend one whole class period completing this first step.
2. Divide the class into small groups.

3. Following are three newspaper articles. Give each student a copy of each article. The students should also have access to a copy of the selection from the *Mishneh Torah*. Using Maimonides' definitions as a guide, ask each group to decide whether any of the articles contain *rechilut* or *lashon hara*. You may also wish to discuss precisely what sort of newspaper would result from strict adherence to Maimonides' guidelines.

   a. NBS television correspondent "X" was arrested and booked for investigation on drunken driving charges, authorities in Chicago, Illinois, said. "X," famous for his series of reports from unusual locations around the world, was halted near Skokie on his way to the airport, early Sunday after a Highway Patrol officer said he spotted "X" in a rented car weaving from lane to lane at about 45 m.p.h. "X," who is now anchorman for the late night news show, is scheduled to appear in court September 25th.

   b. The third wife of author "O" has been granted a June 2nd court hearing on her motion to dismiss her divorce complaint, which was already granted, so she can try to win more alimony and child support money. Mrs. "O" was granted a divorce last June that was to have become final last December 21. But she is asking that the complaint be dismissed because she isn't satisfied with her alimony and child support payments. Probate Judge Angela Burns granted Mrs. "O" $565 a week and cost-of-living increases for seven years, $210 a week for her two daughters and money for their schooling through college.

   c. Television anchorman "M" says he has resigned from Station KNW News because he and other black journalists were routinely excluded from covering major stories. Network spokesperson Arnold Peters said that "M" has not submitted his resignation to KNW officials. "M" told a college audience Sunday night that Black reporters were excluded from covering the presidential inauguration and the return of the hostages. Such omissions are representative of his treatment at KNW, "M" said. The anchorman said he had submitted his resignation because of the omission, but it was refused "for obvious reasons." He is scheduled to meet with network news president Velma Bobbs.

Additional Sources

From the Bible

1. Don't go around gossiping among your people and don't stand idly by the blood of your neighbor.
   Leviticus 19:16

1. לא תלך רכיל בעמיך, לא תעמוד על דם רעך, אני ה׳ (ויקרא יט, טז).

2. The tongue has power over death and life ...
   Proverbs 18:21

2. מות וחיים ביד הלשון (משלי יח, כא).

3. Keep your tongue from evil, your lips from deception.
   Psalms 34:14

3. נצור לשונך מרע, ושפתיך מדבר מרמה (תהילים לד, יד).

4. "... and Joseph brought back to his father a bad report about them ...."
   Genesis 37:2

4. ״ויבא יוסף את דיבתם רעה אל אביהם...״ (בראשית לז, ב).

5. Someone who overlooks an offense is a seeker of love, but someone who repeats the matter loses friends.
   Proverbs 17:9

5. מכסה פשע מבקש אהבה ושנה בדבר מפריד אלוף (משלי יז, ט).

6. If there's no wood the fire will go out and if there's no backbiter a conflict will die out.
   Proverbs 26:20

6. באפס עצים תכבה אש ובאין נרגן ישתוק מדון (משלי כו, כ).

From Rabbinic Literature

1. The world is ruined by eight things: crooked courts, idolatry, incest, murder, profanation of God's name, foul language,

arrogance and scandalmongering.

Seder Eliyahu Rabbah 16

1. בשמונה דברים העולם חרב. על הדינין, ועל העבודה זרה, וגילוי עריות, ושפיכות דמים, וחילול השם, ודברים מכוערים שאדם מוציא מתוך פיו, וגאת הרוח, ולשון הרע....
(סדר אליהו רבה פי, טז).

2. This is the way gossips operate: they start out with something complimentary but finish off with something bad.

Tanchuma (early version), *Shallach*

2. ... כך דרכם של מספרי לשון הרע: פותחים בטובה ומשלימים ברעה... (תנה"ק שלח).

3. Human beings are punished for four things in this world with more [punishment] stored up for them in the world to come: idolatry, incest, and bloodshed — but *lashon hara* equals them all.

J. Peah 1:1

3. ארבעה דברים שהם נפרעין מן האדם בעולם הזה והקרן קיימת לו לעולם הבא: עבודה זרה, וגילוי עריות, ושפיכות דמים – ולשון הרע כנגד כולם,
(ירושי, פאה, פ"א, ה"א).

4. Rav Chisda said that Mar Ukba said: Concerning those who spread *lashon hara,* the Holy One Who is Blessed said: That one and I can't dwell together in the world.

Arachin 15

4. אמר רב חסדא אמר מר עקבא: כל המספר לשון הרע אמר הקדוש ברוך הוא: אין אני והוא יכולים לדור בעולם
(ערכין ט"ו).

5. Anyone who spreads *lashon hara* has no share in the world to come.

Pirke de R. Eliezer 53

5. כל המספר לשון הרע אין לו חלק לעולם הבא
(פדר"א, נ"ג).

6. R. Chama said on the authority of R. Chanina: "What does it mean when it says [lit:] 'Life and death are in the hand of the

tongue.' Does the tongue have a hand? What it means is that just as a hand can kill, so a tongue can kill."

Arachin 15

6. אמר רב חמא ברי חנינא: מהו שנאמר: "מות וחיים ביד הלשון"? וכי יש יד ללשון? לאמר לך מה יד ממיתה אף לשון ממיתה... (ערכי ט"ו).

7. ... *lashon hara* is like the long burning embers of the *rotem* bush, for where as when other embers are extinguished on the outside they're also extinguished on the inside, the *lashon hara* keeps on burning on the inside even if put out on the outside.

Berachot Rabbah 98;
J. Peah 1:1

7. ...גחלי רתמים אף על פי שכבו במחוץ עדיין בוערות מבפנים: כך כל מי שהוא מקבל לשון הרע, אף על פי שאתה הולך ומפייסו והוא מתפייס עדיין הוא בוער מבפנים (ב"ר צח; ירושי פ"א, ה"א).

8. R. Shmuel, the son of Nachman said: Why [in Aramaic] is *lashon hara* called a "third tongue?" Because it kills three: the one who says it, the one who takes it in and the one who is the subject of it ...

Arachin 15; *J. Peah* 1:1,
Deuteronomy Rabbah 5

8. אמר רב שמואל בר נחמן: למה נקרא שמו של לשון הרע לשון שלישי שהוא הורג שלשה: האומרו, והמקבלו, ומי שנאמר עליו...
(ערכי ט"ו; ירושי פאה, פ"א ה"א; דב"ר ה').

9. The tongue is likened to an arrow — why? Because if A unsheathes a sword to kill B and B asks for mercy, A can be mollified and return the sword to its scabbard, but an arrow, once shot cannot be brought back, even if you want to do so."

Saher Tov 120

9. נמשל הלשון לחץ, ולמה? שאם ישלוף האדם והחרב שבידו להרוג את חברו הוא מתחנן לו ומבקש הימנו רחמים, מתנחם החורג ומחזיר החרב לנרתיקה, אבל החץ כיוון שירה אותו והלך, אפילו מבקש להחזיר אינו יכול להחזיר (שו"ט ק"כ).

10. To what can it (*lashon hara*) be compared? ... To a dog who, even though chained up and put behind three separate partitions,

barks and scares everyone. Just think what he would do if he were on the outside! *Lashon hara* is like this: though contained within the mouth and lips it strikes without end. How much more so if it were on the outside! The Holy One, Who is Blessed said, "I can rescue you from any trouble that befalls you, but when it comes to *Lashon hara* you must hide yourself if you are not to suffer from it."

Yalkut Shimoni, Taytzay 23

10. למה הוא דומה (לשון הרע)? לכלב שהוא קשור בשלשלת וחבוש ונתון לפנים משלשה בתים והוא מנפח וכל העם מתייראים ממנו, אלו היה בחוץ מה היה עושה? כך לשון הרע, נתון לפנים מן הפה ולפנים מן השפתיים ומכה שאין לו סוף - אילו היה בחוץ, על אחת כמה וכמה!
אמר הקדוש ברוך הוא: מכל הצרות הבאות עליכם, אני יכול להציל אתכם: אבל בלשון הרע - הטמן עצמך ואין אתה מפסיד (ילק״ש תצא, כ״ג).

11. Resh Lakish said: Some day all animals will gather together, converging on the snake and ask him: "The lion stalks and eats, but what pleasure do you have?" and he (the snake) will reply: "And what pleasure do talebearers have?"

Arachin 15

11. אמר ריש לקיש: מהו שנאמר: ״אם ישך הנחש בלוא לחש ואין יתרון לבעל הלשון״? לעתיד לבוא מתקבצות כל החיות ובאות אצל הנחש ואומרות לו: ארי דורס ואוכל, זאב טורף ואוכל, אתה מה הנאה יש לך? אומר להם: וכי מה יתרון לבעל הלשון? (ערכי ט״ו).

12. R. Shmuel the son of R. Nachman said: ... they said to the snake: How is it that you bite one limb but your poison circulates throughout the body? He (the snake) said to them: "Why are you telling that to me? Tell it to the talebearer who though dwelling in Rome can kill someone in Syria ..."

J. Peah 1:1; *Tanhuma*
(older version) *Chukat;*
Vayikrah Rabbah 26).

12. אמר ר׳ שמואל בר נחמן: אמרו לו לנחש.... ומפני מה אתה נושך באבר אחד וארסך מהלך בכל האיברים? אמר להם: ולי אתם אומרים? אימרו לבעל הלשון, שיושב ברומי והורג בסוריא והורג ברומי (ירוש׳, פאה פ״א, ה״א; תנה״ק חקת; ויק״ר כ״ו).

13. "... they shall be cast before the sword with my people, so strike the thigh [with grief] (Ezekiel 21:17) .... "R. Elazar said: These

are the people who eat and drink with one another while stabbing each other with their sword-like tongues.

Yoma 9

13. "ומגורי אל חרב היו את עמי לכן ספק אל ירך" - אמר ר' אלעזר: אלו בני אדם שאוכלים ושותים זה עם זה ודוקרים זה את זה בחרבות שבלשונם (יומא ט').

14. R. Hisda said that Rabbi Yermiyahu the son of Abba said: Four types of people never behold God's presence: scoffers, liars, hypocrites and those who tell *lashon hara*.

Sanhedrin 103a

14. ואמר רב חסדא אמר רבי ירמיה בר אבא: ארבע כיתות אין מקבלות פני שכינה: כת לצים, כת שקרנים, כת חניפים, כת מספרי לשון הרע (סנה' קג א').

Mishneh Torah: Maimonides

Who is a talebearer?: One who carries gossip, going about from person to person saying: "So-and-so said this; I have heard such-and-such about so-and-so." Even though he tells the truth, he ruins the world. And there is a sin of this type which is even worse, namely: the evil tongue of the scandalmonger who speaks disparagingly of others, even if it's truth. But the one who disparages his neighbor by telling a lie is called a slanderer.

It makes no difference whether a person gossips in the presence or in the absence of the party concerned. Anyone who tells things that, if passed from person to person, are likely to cause physical or financial harm to another person, or even merely to harass or frighten them, is guilty of slander.

All these are scandalmongers and it is forbidden to live among them. It's all the more forbidden to be in their company and hear their talk ....

Hilchot Deot 17:2, 5, 6

משנה תורה:

הלכות דעות, פרק ז' יחידות ב',ה',ו'.

ב. איזהו רכיל? זה שטוען דברים והולך מזה לזה ואומר: כך אמר פלוני, כך וכך שמעתי על פלוני אף על פי שהוא אומר אמת; הרי זה מחריב את העולם. יש עוון גדול מזה עד מאוד והוא בגלל לאוו זה, והוא לשון הרע והוא מספר בגנות חברו, אף על פי שאמר אמת אבל האומר שקר נקרא מוציא שם רע על חברו....

ה. אחד המספר בלשון הרע בפני חברו או שלא בפניו,
והמספר דברים שגומרים אם נשמעו איש מפי איש;
להזיק חברו בגופו או בממונו, ואפילו להצר לו
או להפחידו, הרי זה לשון הרע....

ו. כל אלו הם בעלי לשון הרע שאסור לדור בשכנותם,
וכל שכן לשב עמהם ולשמוע דבריהם....

From Rabbenu Yonah of Gerona (1201-1263):

CCXV. Know that if one sees his neighbor transgressing a commandment of the Torah in secret, and he makes his sins public, his guilt is very great. For perhaps the sinner has repented of his evil way and is troubled in his thoughts. ("The heart knows its own bitterness.") It is proper to reveal them only to a discreet sage, who will not pass them on to others. One should keep himself from his company until it becomes known to him that he has repented of his evil way. And if the sinner is a Torah scholar and one who fears sin, it should be assumed that he has indeed repented, and that though his evil inclination may have overpowered him once, he is bitter in consequence.

CCXVI. There are two evils attaching to the slanderer: the injury and the shame which he causes his neighbor, and his choosing to render him reprehensible and iniquitous and to rejoice over his misfortune. In one respect the transgression of one who slanders through the truth is greater than that of one who slanders through falsehood; for people will believe the first in that what he says of his neighbor rings of the truth. And the one who is so spoken of will appear despicable to them and will be despised by them after having regretted his evil and having been forgiven for his sins.

Gates of Repentance by Rabbi Yonah of Gerona (Jerusalem: Philipp Feldheim, Inc. 1967), Part 3, Paragraphs 215, 216

שערי תשובה, (רי יונה גירונדי) שער שלישי, רטייו-רטייז:

רטו. ודע, כי אם יראה איש כי עבר חברו על דבר-תורה
בסתר והוא גלה על חטאתיו על שער-בת-רבים, אשם
אשם על זה, כי אולי החוטא ההוא שב מדרכו הרעה,
ויגוניו ברעיוניו, ולב יודע מרת נפשו. ולא

נכון לגלותם זולתי לחכם צנוע אשר לא יספר ליתר ההמון, רק הרחק ירחיק מחברתו עד אשר יודע אליו כי שב מדרכו הרעה. ואם החוטא תלמיד-חכם ואיש ירא-חטא, ראוי לחשוב עליו כי באמת עשה תשובה, ואם יתקפו יצרו פעם אחת, נפשו מרה לו אחרי-כן.

רטז. והמספר לשון הרע, שתים הנה קוראותיו, הנזק והבשת אשר יגרום לחברו, ובחירתו לחיב ולהרשיע את חבריו, ושמחתו לאידם. ועל צד אחד יגדל עון המספר לשון הרע על דבר אחת מן המספר על דבר שקר, כי יאמין העם בספרו על חברו דברים כנים, ויעלה באשו לפניהם, ויהיה לבוז בעיניהם, אחר אשר נחם על רעתו ונסלח לו מחטאותיו.

4th Grade – 6th Grade

UNIT VI — The Scapegoat

שעיר המשתלח

1. Introduction for the Teacher
2. Dilemma Story
3. Suggested Procedure and Cue Sheet
4. Supplementary Exercises
5. Additional Sources

About This Unit

The subject of this unit is how one's own sins often come to be viewed as the fault of others.

From a biblical perspective, *scapegoating* is a primordial human defence mechanism. Adam scapegoats Eve; Eve scapegoats the snake. Cain scapegoats God ("Am *I* my brother's protector?"); the Israelites scapegoat Moses ... primordial indeed.

In discussing this unit's dilemma, students reasoning at Stage 2 may seek to justify isolating the "scapegoat" on the basis of "self-preservation." Students reasoning at Stage 3, however, will tend to condemn such a justification as "mean," and will distance themselves from anything disapproved of by parents or teachers.

Introduction for the Teacher

"It's typical of human beings that anger in one's household comes to rest upon the littlest member ..."

Mechilta, De-Vayissa, 7

״דרך ארץ אדם כועס בתוך ביתו אינו נותן עיניו אלא בקטן...״ (מכילתא דויסע ז׳).

Some common human psychological processes work at cross-purposes with rational and socially functional moral decision making. One such process is commonly referred to as scapegoating. Simply put, scapegoating means the shirking of responsibility for one's own misfortunes by shifting the blame to others.

> An infant when balked will kick and scream ... The infant attacks not the true source of the frustration, but any object or person who crosses its path.

> Throughout life the same tendency persists for anger to center upon available rather than upon logical objects. Everyday speech recognizes this *displacement* in a variety of phrases: to take it out on the dog; don't take it out on me; whipping boy; scapegoat.[1]

Scapegoating is an attempt to purge oneself of displeasurable feelings and responsibilities, and thus possess a certain internal logic. This logic, however, is negated by the dual dysfunctions of the process: (1) It makes victims of people who have little or nothing to do with causing the displeasure that one is seeking to avoid, and (2) It fails to deal with the actual cause of one's distress.

In choosing scapegoats, we tend to look for persons with characteristics which we can most easily rationalize as making one deserving of blame. Possession of physical, psychological or social traits which are generally thought of as undesirable in a given social group leave one much more vulnerable to being scapegoated. As part of this unit's initial development, I asked two of my classes to describe the scapegoated character in this unit's dilemma story. Both classes volunteered long and rather detailed lists of scapegoat-inviting characteristics, in effect sketching for me a portrait of the ideal scapegoat.

In this unit's dilemma story, a child is presented with the opportunity of helping place the responsibility for the problems of an entire class in the lap of one unpopular classmate. The dilemma awaits your class' solution.

Dilemma Story

Script for "THE SCAPEGOAT"

Mike: I'm in kind of a tough situation. I have a hard decision to make. I want you to listen to three different people describe what happened in class this morning and then I'll tell you about my decision. First, there's Carrie's description of what happened.

Carrie: We have a really noisy class. Today we were especially bad. Halfway through the class the teacher got so mad she said that if anyone interrupted her again we would all lose our free time. Right before class ended, Brian started complaining about the kid sitting next to him. Brian said he was writing things about him on his desk. Brian is always whining about something, but the teacher likes him because he's such a goody-goody. Anyway, the teacher said that that was the last straw; free time was cancelled. *I* think only Brian should lose *his* free time because if it weren't for him, all of us would have still gotten ours. The teacher's been taking away a lot of fun stuff lately and it's not fair that we're all punished just because of Brian. He's always ruining things — that's why nobody likes him.

Mike: Now here's Brian's description of what happened this morning.

Brian: Our teacher was having a bad day. She got really upset at our talking and interrupting. I'm always very careful not to disturb the class, but I was especially careful today because the teacher said that the next time she was interrupted everyone would lose their free time.

A couple minutes before class ended, I noticed that Alan was writing something dirty about me on his desk, so I said: "Hey! Stop writing stuff about me!"

He didn't stop, so I tried to show the teacher what he was writing so that *she* would make him stop. Alan whispered that I should be quiet or we'd lose our free time, but I was really mad at him always picking on me like this, so I kept trying to get the teacher's attention. Well, the teacher didn't help me either. She said that that was the last straw and that there would be no free time today.

I guess I did interrupt, but it wasn't my fault.

Teacher: The class was quite disruptive today; Jim, Alan, Lisa, Brian and Carrie in particular. I guess they were really getting to me because about halfway through the class I said that if I were interrupted again everyone would lose their free time. A few minutes before free time usually begins, one of the kids, Brian, started complaining about something. Brian's an unpopular child and it's not unusual for him to be in the middle of some kind of problem, or complaining about something. The more popular kids think that Brian's weird and don't have much to do with him. I didn't want to blame Brian — it seemed a little unfair — but I was tired and frustrated and really didn't have much choice.

Mike: Well, now you should have an idea of what happened in class today. Here's my problem: Carrie just called and said that she was fed up with Brian always ruining things, and that if the teacher wouldn't stop Brian from messing things up, the students should. She said she was starting a "Stop Brian for the Sake of the Class Club" and she asked me to join. Carrie said that even if the club couldn't stop Brian from messing things up, it was important that we all join to show Brian that we were against his ruining things all the time.

Should I join?

Suggested Procedure

1. This unit is designed to be presented as a tape recorded "radio play." It has four roles, three for children and one for an adult. If you decide to present the story as a play, try to choose actors whose voices your students will *not* recognize so that the actors' actual identities are not confused with the issues raised by the dilemma. If you don't want to present the dilemma as a play, you may want to introduce the story by explaining that it will be told by four different people, each in the first person.
2. Explain that you are going to read (or play a tape that tells) a story. At the end of the story the class will be asked a question, so they must listen carefully. Then play the tape (or read the story).
3. Give the students a minute or so to think about their answer to the question that concludes the story, then poll them. (You may wish to make the poll anonymous by taking a paper ballot — some class members might be shy about expressing their true feelings if they feel "outnumbered" or on the "wrong side.")
4. Discuss the results of the poll, alternating between students who disagree about the proper solution to the dilemma. You may wish to interject the following questions to stimulate discussion:
   a. Who caused the class to lose their recess?
   b. What would be the result of removing Brian from the class?
   c. If it had been Carrie's interruption that was the "last straw," do you think a "Stop Carrie for the Sake of the Class" club would have been started? Why?
   d. Are whole groups of people ever treated like the class treated Brian? Give examples.
5. Poll the class a second time.

Cue Sheet

Below, on the left, are some points your students might bring up in the course of discussing this unit's dilemma. On the right you'll find some suggested responses to these comments. These critical responses are designed to help focus discussion on possible weaknesses or contradictions in the reasoning which led to the initial comment. It is most often preferable that these sorts of responses come from other classmates, but if such challenges are not forthcoming, you yourself should provide them.

Student Statements	Possible Teacher Response
1. I don't think the club would help much, but Mike should be loyal to his friends, so he should join.	1. What if Brian was also Mike's friend? Which loyalty comes first — Mike's loyalty to the group or to Brian?
2. They're just picking on Brian because he's unpopular.	2. But Brian *does* misbehave. Just because he's unpopular is no reason to excuse him for getting into trouble. A fair solution to the problem must deal with everyone's behavior.
3. If the other students don't teach Brian a lesson, he'll just continue to misbehave.	3. But several other students were also misbehaving. Why should Brian be singled out for punishment? Would you join a "Stop Carrie Club" if Brian was the one who called you?
4. If the other students were nice to Brian, maybe he wouldn't act that way anymore.	4. What if you tried to be nice to Brian, but the class continued to end up in trouble? Would you *then* join the club? If sticking up for Brian meant losing your other friends, would you still do it?
5. If all the other students began a "Stop Brian Club," the teacher would see that they were trying to be good.	5. Misbehavior should be dealt with by teachers — not other students. If the students started trying to handle problems like this one, it would just end up making everyone angrier and less cooperative.

Supplementary Exercises

1. A careful reading of the biblical story of Joseph and his brothers (Genesis 37-50) reveals the scapegoating process as one of this narrative's major themes. There are many similarities between Joseph's story and this unit's dilemma play, e.g., both Joseph's

and Brian's peers consider them favored and pampered by adults; both are described as being tattletales; both are conspired against by their peers, etc.

Reading all or part of the Joseph narrative with your class is one way of further exploring the moral dilemma raised in this unit. In reading the Joseph story you may point out, or even list, those points which are common to both stories. You may also wish to discuss whether the conclusion of the story of Joseph and his brothers supplies any clues as to how scapegoating relationships can best be overcome.

2. Read Leviticus 16:3-22. It describes a ritual which took place in the *Bet HaMikdash* each Yom Kippur. The term scapegoat has its origin in this ritual. As part of a follow-up lesson to this unit's dilemma story, you may wish to use this reference in explaining the origin of the term scapegoat to your class.

Additional Sources

1. Don't give any credence to someone who speaks badly of others, except for a teacher who tells such things to his students so they don't do likewise. In fact, anyone who attributes evil to others can be suspect concerning that very evil. As the saying goes, "The one who finds flaws is flawed, and the fault he finds is his own." Why does the saying go, "the fault he finds is his own?" Because a fault finder can only find fault by attributing to others what is actually true of himself.

Sefer Hasidim, Section 632

ספר חסידים, פרק תרל״ב

אדם שמספר רע על בני אדם אל תכריעו אלא הרב מספר לתלמידיו כדי שלא יעשו כך ודע שכל המספר על בני אדם רע תוכל לחשדו בדבר זה רע שמספר על אחרים שהרי אמרו כל הפוסל פסול ובמומו הוא פוסל ולמה אמרו במומו הוא פוסל כי הלב של הפוסל לא יוכל לחשוב מום לחבירו אלא במה שמצוי בו אומר לאחרים.

2. Further References

Allport, Gordon. *The Nature of Prejudice,*New York, Anchor Books Edition, 1958.

Ryan, W. *Blaming the Victim*, New York: Vintage Books, 1971.

Zeligs, Ruth. *Psychoanalysis and the Bible*. New York: Bloch Publishing Co., 1974. (A psychoanalytical examination of the Joseph narrative)

4th Grade – 7th Grade

UNIT VII — Deception

גנבת דעת

1. Introduction for the Teacher
2. Dilemma Story
3. Suggested Procedure and Cue Sheet
4. Supplementary Exercise
5. Additional Sources

About This Unit

The Hebrew term *g'nevat da'at* (literally, opinion stealing) refers to a whole range of activities which result in someone being deceived. This unit deals with *g'nevat da'at* and its potential consequences.

At different stages of moral judgment a given act of deception can be understood in very different ways. This unit is designed for use in the intermediate grades, where students will most likely deal with *g'nevat da'at* on the basis of naive reciprocity — "I have the right to deceive someone who is being unfair to me" (Stage 2); what is expected of one by others "A good Jew doesn't lie" (Stage 3); or one's duty to society — "What if everybody lied?" (Stage 4).

Introduction for the Teacher

The human beings that God placed in the Garden of Eden were *arumim* (means both "naked" and "cunning") like the snake.[1] *Targum Yonatan* understands this double use of *arum* as an allusion to the wily nature of all three characters — the man, the woman and the snake.[2] At any rate, we can't be far from the mark if we conclude that the evasion and dissemblance to which the man and woman resort in avoiding the question "Have you eaten from the tree ... what have you done ... ?"[3] should be understood as typically human.

Like our prototypes in the garden, we learn while still young how to use our wits to deceive. In acquiring these skills of deception, we transform "telling the truth" into a calculated act. We learn to shape the truth we tell. We render it a work of art —the primal work of art.

The art of telling the truth is the subject of this unit's dilemma story. The story operates on three levels. On the first level, it is a story about copying from a classmate's test. Entry to the story's second level is through its reference to Genesis Chapter 20, which deals with Abraham's sojourn in Gerar. You will remember that this passage centers on an act of deception (see Supplementary Exercise). The third level of the dilemma involves comparing the comments of three classic medieval exegetes, Ramban, Ibn Ezra and Sforno, who come to significantly different conclusions about Abraham's conduct in Gerar. It is this disagreement which brings the dilemma story full circle by providing us with the three suggested solutions for the dilemma.

Dilemma Story

Stephanie was absent from Bible class yesterday. The subject of yesterday's lesson was the twentieth chapter of Genesis, which describes a visit that Abraham and Sarah made to a place called Gerar. At the end of the lesson, the teacher told the class that there would be a test the next day on what happened to Abraham and Sarah in Gerar.

Today Stephanie is back in class. Sandy, her close friend, is trying to fill her in quickly on what she missed yesterday. Meanwhile, the teacher is beginning to hand out paper for the test. Stephanie, realizing that the test is going to be about a lesson she missed, raises her hand and says: "I'm not prepared to take the test because I was absent yesterday."

The teacher replies: "I know you were absent yesterday, Stephanie, but I can't give the test to each of you individually. The only other time you could take it would be on Friday, during the school picnic."

Stephanie decides to take the test now, rather than during the picnic. She's guessing at some answers, but #4 really has her stumped. That question reads: "What's the name of the place that Abraham and Sarah visited?" Stephanie glances over at Sandra's paper and notices that her answer to #4 is: "The place is called Avimelech."

On her paper Stephanie writes: "The place they visited is called Avimelech."

The students have now completed their tests and are handing them in. Later, while going over the tests, the teacher notices that on question #4, Sandra has made the mistake of confusing the name of the king of Gerar, which was Avimelech, with the name of the place itself. Now she notices that Stephanie has made the same mistake. The teacher thinks: "It's strange that both Stephanie and Sandra would make this same mistake. They're such good friends

—I wonder ... "The teacher calls Stephanie up to her desk and asks her: 'Stephanie, did you copy Sandra's test?'"

Stephanie considers three possible answers to the teacher's question:

1. I should say "no" (I didn't copy) because it wasn't fair to have to take the test when I was unprepared or else miss the picnic.
2. I should say "yes" (I did copy).
3. I should say "no" (I didn't copy) because I didn't actually copy Sandra's paper. I just used part of it.

Which of these three answers do you think Stephanie should give the teacher?

Suggested Procedure

1. Present the dilemma story.
2. Have each student choose what they think to be the best response/rationale for Stephanie's dilemma from among the three possible solutions provided at the end of the story.
3. Poll the students on which answer each has chosen.
4. Have each student explain why he or she chose their particular solution, alternating between students who have chosen different answers.
5. To help stimulate and direct the discussion, you may wish to use these follow-up questions:
   a. What is worse — to mislead someone or to allow them to mislead you?
   b. Have you ever been glad you were misled? Explain.
   c. (For students who chose solution 1 or 3) Would you call your solution "lying?" If yes, are you saying that telling a lie is the best thing to do in this situation?
   d. Is it lying to answer a question in a way that you're quite certain the other person won't understand? For instance: "Okay" means the same thing as "maybe" to you. Someone asks you to do them a favor. You say "okay." The other person thinks your answer means yes, but you meant maybe. Is this lying?
6. Be sure to explore the most likely consequences of each of the three solutions: Ask "What if ..." questions based on each of the three solutions.
7. Do the Supplementary Exercise.

Cue Sheet

Below, on the left, are some points your students might bring up in the course of discussing this unit's dilemma. On the right you'll find some suggested responses to these comments. These critical responses are designed to help focus discussion on possible weaknesses or contradictions in the reasoning which led to the initial comment. It is most often preferable that these sorts of responses come from other classmates, but if such challenges are not forthcoming, you yourself should provide them.

Student Statements	Possible Teacher Response
1. It's not a good idea to mislead the teacher, because if you get caught, you'll be in worse trouble.	1 But if you could be sure that you wouldn't be caught, would it be okay, or are there any other good reasons you can think of for telling the teacher the truth?
2. I'd say I copied, but I'd tell the teacher that the whole thing wasn't fair.	2. What does one thing have to do with the other? Don't you owe it to yourself *and* the teacher to be honest with her? Wouldn't you want her to be honest with you?
3. In my own mind I know I'm not lying if I say I didn't copy, because to me copying means having the same answer *word for word.*	3. If everyone simply had to convince *themselves* that they weren't lying, nobody could be sure what anyone meant about anything.
4. I'd say that I didn't copy. Just because the teacher is being unfair to me doesn't mean that I shoud have to miss the picnic.	4. What if the teacher found out and never quite trusted you again?

5. It's not nice to lie, and I'd feel especially bad lying to a teacher.

5. If someone whispered something mean about the teacher to you and the teacher asked you what that person whispered, would you tell the teacher? In such a case, would you feel bad about misleading the teacher? What if you really liked/disliked the whisperer? What if you really liked/disliked the teacher?

Supplementary Exercise

Chapter 20 of Genesis is referred to in this dilemma story. In fact, the dilemma story is this passage in disguise. Both stories deal with whether or not there are situations in which one might be justified in misleading others. Have students read Genesis 20.

Below are excerpts from three biblical commentaries dealing with Abraham's behavior in this incident. Two of these three commentaries exonerate Abraham, while the third finds his behavior inexcusable. You may wish to read and discuss this passage and the accompanying commentaries with your class. The following questions may help to direct the discussion:

1. Which commentary do you find most convincing? Why?
2. Does it make a difference that Abraham believed that his life was at stake?
3. Did Sarah have a responsibility in the matter which was distinct from that of Abraham?

Ramban on Genesis 20:12

I know of no good reason for this excuse, even though it was true that she was his sister *and* his wife. When they wanted the woman he said to them, "She's my sister" to mislead them, thereby wronging them by bringing upon them a great sin. It makes absolutely no difference whether it's true or not ...

1. רמב״ן

לא ידעתי טעם להתנצלות הזה כי גם אם אמת הדבר שהיתה אחותו ואשתו וברצותם באשה אמר להם אחותי היא להטעותם בדבר כבר חטא בהם להביא עליהם חטאה גדולה ואין חלוק והפרש כלל בין שהדבר אמת או שקר.

Ibn Ezra on Genesis 20:12

It seems to me that he was less than frank with Avimelech because circumstances demanded it. See "I'm Esau your firstborn" (Genesis 27:19): These are spiritual words [matters?], for the prophets can be divided into two types. The first type is a medium for commandments. The second type predicts the future, and if they need to say something which isn't exactly accurate it does no harm. The medium for commandments, however, may not mislead at all. Consider David. He is referred to as "the man of God," and he said, "The spirit of God communed with me." He didn't level with Avimelech ... because circumstances demanded it. Also Elisha in speaking to Hazael ... and Micaiah who uttered an empty prayer ... Likewise, Abraham said, "And besides, she really is my sister," and "We will worship and we will return" (Genesis 22:5).

2. אבן עזרא

.... אברהם דחה אבימלך בדברים כפי צורך השעה...
"אנכי עשו בכורך"
.... ואלה דברי רוח כי הנביאים יתחלקו לבי חלקים;
החלק הראשון שליח במצוות והחלק השני נביאי העתיד
ואם יצטרכו לאמר דבר שאיננו כהוגן לא יזיק, רק
השליח לא יתכן שיכזב כלל. גם הנה דוד... בלבל
דבריו עם אחימלך... גם אלישע שאמר לחזאל... וכן
מכיהו אמר תפילה שוא... דרך מוסר. וכן אמר אברהם
"וגם אמנה" ו"נשתחווה ונשובה."

Sforno on Genesis 20:12

You, the most righteous of kings, have sinned in this matter, since you took the woman because I said that she was my sister. It was up to you to ask if she was also my wife; as she is, in fact, my sister *and* my wife.

3. ספורנו

וגם אתה המלך הצדיק בהם חטאת בזה שלקחת האשה
בשביל שאמרתי שהיא אחותי שהיה לך לשאול אם היא
גם כן אשתי כמו שהיא באמת אחותי ואשתי.

Additional Sources

1. The Rabbinic term *g'nevat da'at (opinion stealing) is equivalent to the biblical g'nevat lev* (heart stealing)."לב"in the Bible is often best understood as *mind* or *spirit* and is in this sense conceived of as the seat of wisdom.

The term *g'nevat lev* is used three times in the Bible, twice in connection with Jacob (Genesis 31) and once in connection with Absalom (see II Samuel 15). *G'nevat lev* is, in fact, the dominant theme of Genesis 31, the root גנב appearing seven times in the chapter. The passage is drenched with duplicity as Jacob, Rachel and Laban are all shown to be playing the game of *g'nevat da'at*. This same dissembling spirit also permeates II Samuel 15, which describes Absalom's campaign to gain his father's throne. You may wish to examine one or both of these passages with your class as part of your ongoing discussion of *g'nevat da'at*.

2. Do not steal, nor deceive, nor lie to one another, and do not swear falsely by my name, profaning the name of your God — I am the Lord ... Do not curse the deaf nor put an obstacle before the blind — You will fear your God, I am the Lord.
   Leviticus 19:11, 12, 14

   a. Rashi (Leviticus 19:11, 12): If you steal you will end up deceiving, which will lead to lying, which will lead to swearing falsely (19:14). "... and before the blind ...": Do not give a person who is "blind" in a matter advice which is improper to him/her ... "And you will fear your God": Since human beings are not capable of knowing whether such a person's intentions are for good or evil, as one could always say: "I meant it for the best," it is therefore stated, "and you will fear your God." He knows your thought.
   b. *Sifte chachamim*, commenting on the phrase "and before the blind": In other words, don't try to trick him ("trick" in the sense of being *sly*) ... by plotting. It's like ripping someone off, as in "he's ripped me off twice" (Genesis 37:36).

2. לא תגנבו ולא תכחשו ולא תשקרו איש בעמיתו ולא תשבעו בשמי לשקר וחללת את שם אלוהים אני ה'.... לא תקלל חרש ולפני עוור לא תיתן מכשול ויראת מאלוהיך אני ה'. (ויקרא יט: יא, יב, יד).

א. רש"י - (י"א, י"ב) אם גנבת סופך לכחש סופך לשקר סופך להשבע לשקר... (י"ד).
"ולפני עוור": לפני הסומא בדבר לא תיתן עצה שאינה הוגנת לו, "ויראת מאלוהיך": ולפי שהדבר הזה אינו מסור לבריות לידענו. אם דעתו של זה לטובה או לרעה ויכול להשמט ולאמר לטובה נתכוונתי לפיכך נאמר בו "ויראת מאלוהיך" - המכיר מחשבותיך.

ב. פירוש שפתי חכמים: "לפני עוור": כמו אל תבוא עליו בעקיפין (ולשון ערמה הוא)... בעלילות, והוא כמו עוקב, ל"ויעקבני זה פעמים".

3. One of the most important elements in the Joseph narrative (Genesis 37-50) is the dramatic unfolding of two deliberate and intertwined acts of deception:
   a. The brothers deceiving their father concerning the true fate of Joseph, and
   b. Joseph deceiving his brothers as to his true identity. You may wish to explore this complex web of *g'nevat da'at* with your students.

From Rabbinic Literature

1. Our Rabbis taught: How does one dance before a bride? Bet Shamai says: (Praise of) the bride should be as she is, and Bet Hillel says: "What a beautiful and graceful bride!"

   Bet Shammai said to Bet Hillel: If she was lame or blind does one say of her "What a beautiful and graceful bride?" Doesn't the Torah say "Stay far away from falsehood?" Bet Hillel said to Bet Shammai: According to your view, if one has made a bad purchase in the market, should another praise it or criticize it? Surely, one should praise it. It is for this reason that the sages taught: one should always have a pleasant disposition toward others.

Ketubot 16b, 17a

1. תנו רבנן:
כיצד מרקדין לפני הכלה? בית שמאי אומרים כלה כמות שהיא ובית הלל אומרים כלה נאה וחסודה. אמרו להן ב״ש לב״ה הרי שהיתה חיגרת או סומא אומרים לה כלה נאה וחסודה?-- והתורה אמרה מדבר שקר תרחק. אמרו להם ב״ה לב״ש לדבריכם מי שלקח מקח רע מן השוק ישבחנו בעיניו או יגננו בעיניו? הווי אומר ישבחנו בעיניו. מכאן אמרו חכמים לעולם תהי דעתו של אדם מעורבת עם הבריות (כתובות ט״ז; י״ז).

2. There are seven types of thieves but a "thought thief" (one who deceives another) is the worst of all.

Mechilta, Mishpatim Chapter 13, Paragraph 135

2. שבעה גנבים הם, הראשון שבגנבים -- גונב דעת הבריות (מכילתא, משפטים).

3. Shmuel said: It's forbidden to deceive someone, even if the other person isn't a Jew.

Chulin 94

3. אמר שמואל: אסור לגנוב דעת הבריות, ואפילו דעתו של נכרי (חולין, צ״ד).

4. Mar Zutra, the son of R. Nachman, was walking from Sirca to Be M'huza at the same time that Rava and R. Sifra were walking to Sirca. They met. Mar Zutra concluded that they (Rava and R. Sifra) were on their way to meet him and so he said to them: Why have you scholars bothered to walk all this way? R. Sifra said to him: We didn't know that you were coming, sir. Had we known, we would have put ourselves out more than this. Rava said to R. Sifra: Why did you tell him that and upset him? He replied: We would have misled him otherwise. (Rava said): No. He would have been misleading himself.

Chulin 94

4. מר זוטרא בנו של רב נחמן היה מהלך מסירכא לבי מחוזא ורבא ורב ספרא היו מהלכים לסירכא. פגעו זה בזה. כסבור מר זוטרא שלקראתו הם יוצאים, אמר להם: מה להם לחכמים שטרחו לילך כלכך? אמר לו רב ספרא: אנו לא היינו יודעים שבא מר, אלו היינו יודעים היינו טורחים יותר. אמר רבא לרב ספרא: מפני מה אמרת לו כך והחלשת דעתו? אמר לו: והרי היינו מטעים אותו. הוא הוא שהיה מטעה את עצמו (חולין, צ״ד).

5. You must have a just *ephah* and a just *hin* (Leviticus 19:36) — R. Yose the son of R. Yehudah said: What does this passage mean, "a just *hin*"? Isn't the (measure) *hin* included in the category of the (measure) *ephah*? Rather, this passage means that one's *hin* (Aramaic for "yes") should be honest and one's "no" should be honest.

Baba Mezia 59

5. ״איפת צדק והין צדק יהיה לכם״ אמר ר׳ יוסי ברי יהודה: מה תלמוד לאמר: ״הין צדק״, והלא הין בכלל איפה הוא? אלא לאמר לך שיהא ״הין״ שלך צדק ו״לאו״ שלך צדק (ב״מ, נ״ט).

6. This is the punishment of a liar — even when they tell the truth nobody listens to them.

Sanhedrin 89

6. כך ענשו של בדאי -- שאפילו אומר אמת אין שומעין לו (סנהי פייט).

7. Chizkiah said: How do we know that whoever adds (to the word of God) detracts from it? Because it is said: "God said, 'Don't eat from it *and don't touch it*,'" (Genesis 3:3). In God's directions to the man, no mention was made of *touching* the tree. Thus, when the human beings touched the tree and nothing happened, the serpent could counter, "I thought you said you couldn't even touch it!"

Sanhedrin 29

7. אמר חזקיה: מנין שכל המוסיף גורע? שנאמר: אמר אלוהים לא תאכלו ממנו ולא תגעו בו (סנהי כייט).

8. Teach your tongue to say "I don't know" — lest you be caught making something up.

Brachot 4

8. למד לשונך לאמר ״אינ י יודע״ -- שמא תתבדה ותאחז (ברי, די).

9. The Holy One Who is Blessed is an adversary of anyone who says one thing with the mouth but something else in the heart.

Pesachim 113

9. המדבר אחד בפה ואחד בלב -- הקדוש ברוך הוא שונאו (פסחי קייג).

10. "Yes, yes" constitutes a vow — "No, no" constitutes a vow.

Shavuot 36

10. הן הן שבועה -- לאו לאו שבועה (שבועות לייו).

From *Sefer Hasidim*

It's forbidden to flatter or seduce, saying one thing with one's mouth while thinking something else in one' s heart. One should say what one actually thinks. Furthermore, it is forbidden to deceive anyone, even a non-Jew; those people who insult non-Jews while appearing to greet them, the non-Jew understanding what he said to him as a greeting, are sinners, for there is no greater deception than this ...

Sefer Hasidim 51

״ספר חסידים״:

אסור להנהיג עצמו בדברי חלקות ופיתוי ולא ידבר אחד בפה ואחד בלב. אלא תוכו כפיו והעניין שבלב הוא הדבר שבפה. ואסור לגנוב דעת הבריות ואפילו דעתו של גוי ואותן שמחרפין את הגויים בשעת שאלת שלומם והגוי סבור שאמר לו טובה חוטאים כי אין לך גניבת דעת גדול מזה.... (נ״א).

From the *Shulchan Aruch*

It is forbidden to employ misleading business practices or to deceive someone, e.g., if one's goods are damaged one must inform the buyer, even if he is an idolator, and one may not sell him unkosher meat while giving the impression that it is kosher. It is even forbidden to mislead someone by appearing to do something on his behalf when in fact one is not doing so. How, for instance? By insisting that someone join you for dinner though you know that he will refuse or by offering lots of refreshments that you know he will not accept. One also may not give him the impression that you're opening new casks (of wine) for him when in fact they've been open for (inspection by) a merchant; you must inform him that they were not opened on his account ... however, if he mislead *himself*, thinking that something has been done in his honor when, in fact, it was not, e.g., meeting someone on the road who is under the impression that you've come out to greet him (but you have not) you needn't inform him.

Hoshen Mishpat 228:6

אסור לרמות בני אדם במקח וממכר או לגנוב דעתם ככון אם יש מום במקחו צריך להודיעו ללוקח אף אם הוא עכו״ם. לא ימכור לו בשר נבילה בחזקת שחוטה. ואף לגנוב דעת הבריות בדברים שמראה שעושה בשבילו ואינו עושה אסור. כיצד? לא יסרהב (בחבירו) שיסעוד עמו והוא יודע שאינו סועד ולא ירבה לו בתקרובי׳ והוא יודע שאינו מקבל. ולא יפתח חביות הפתוחות לחנווני וזה סובר שפתחם בשבילו, אלא צריך להודיעו שלא פתחם בשבילו. ואם הוא דבר דאיבעי׳ ליה לאסוקי אדעתיה שאינו עושה בשבילו ומטעה עצמו שסובר שעושה בשבילו

לכבודו כגון שפגע בחבירו בדרך וסבור זה שיצא לקראתו
לכבודו אין צריך להודיעו. (שולחן ערוך, חשן המשפט
רכ״ח:ו׳).

Another Source

Jacob, Louis. *Jewish Biblical Exegesis* (Chain of Tradition Series, Vol IV). New York: Behrman House, 1973.

Chapter 19 of this collection of excerpts from Jewish exegetical classics is a selection from Baruch Epstein's *Torah T'mimah* which deals with *g'nevat da'at*.

5th Grade – 7th Grade

UNIT VIII — Revenge
נקמה

1. Introduction for the Teacher
2. Dilemma Story
3. Suggested Procedure and Cue Sheet
4. Supplementary Exercise
5. Additional Sources

About This Unit

In previous units, we have explored how Stage 2 moral reasoning emphasizes *fairness* (everyone getting an equal share) and an "enlightened self-interest." In this unit we examine a corollary of Stage 2 fairness: you need deal fairly with others only as long as they respond fairly to you.

This unit's dilemma story deals with revenge. Stage 2 thinkers may or may not justify revenge as the proper response to this unit's dilemma question, but they will, in either case, base their decision on some notion of reciprocity and self-interest. In contrast, Stage 3 thinkers will be preoccupied with how an act of revenge might be perceived by "significant others" (parents, friends, teachers, etc.). Unlike either Stage 2 or 3 thinkers, children reasoning at Stage 4 will express concern for the social consequences of vengeance *or* forbearance ("What if everybody acted vengefully?"; "What if nobody acted vengefully?").

Introduction for the Teacher

There is no need for *mitzvot* which prescribe totally instinctual and inevitable behavior. On the contrary, *mitzvot* tend to call for actions which would otherwise be unlikely. In a moral context, certain *mitzvot* function as conduits which redirect instinctual, indiscriminate impulses towards actions that are socially constructive. This unit deals with one such impulse: revenge.

In exploring this dilemma with your class you may wish to deal with the following issues:

1. What social impact do acts of vengeance have?
2. What social impact does non-retaliation have?

3. How should one respond to new provocation by old offenders who have never tried to change their ways?
4. What effects might each of the solutions which are found at the end of the dilemma have on the individuals who are directly involved?
5. Do the students distinguish between what they *would* do and what they *should* do?

Dilemma Story

Joanne is not well thought of by her classmates. She pulls all kinds of stunts to get attention, but never seems to get caught or to be held responsible for her actions. Once, for instance, she was throwing spitballs in class, but *you* were blamed for it. She let you get punished for the spitballs without confessing that it was she who had thrown them. On another occasion she hid your friend Bonnie's boots and Bonnie had to walk home through the snow without them. However, Joanne's behavior was not affected by how others treated her in return. This was so regardless of whether they tried to remain friendly or tried to "teach her a lesson" by acting towards her as she did towards them.

One morning Joanne's book bag disappears. Joanne tells everyone that she thinks someone is hiding it and that she needs her books to study for an important math test tomorrow. But the book bag remains missing throughout the day.

After school as you start home, you notice Joanne's book bag stuffed behind the school garbage bin. Joanne, who is already on her bus, sees you looking behind the garbage bin. The bus is about to leave so she can't get off, but she calls to you, "Is my book bag behind there?"

Bonnie, who is walking with you says, "Don't tell her! Remember the spitballs and my boots. She never gets caught when *she* does things to *us*. Let her see how it feels for a change."

If you choose to do so, you could hand Joanne the book bag through the window before the bus leaves. What do you do?

a. Bring her the bag.
b. Say to Joanne, "I'm not going to help you. It's your own fault your bag is missing."
c. Pretend that you didn't hear her.

Suggested Procedure

1. Read the dilemma story with the class.
2. Poll each student as to which solution he or she perfers.

3. Have the students explain why they chose their respective solutions. It may help to stimulate discussion if you alternate between students who prefer different solutions.
4. Poll the students again to see if any have changed their minds.
5. Do the supplementary exercise.
6. Examine one of the supplementary texts provided in the additional sources.

Cue Sheet

Below, on the left, are some points your students might bring up in the course of discussing this unit's dilemma. On the right you'll find some suggested responses to these comments. These critical responses are designed to help focus discussion on possible weaknesses or contradictions in the reasoning which led to the initial comment. It is most often preferable that these sorts of responses come from other classmates, but if such challenges are not forthcoming, you yourself should provide them.

Student Statements	Possible Teacher Response
1. I'd treat her the way she had treated me, because it would make me feel good to get back at her.	1. What if doing that made other people think less of you?
2. She should see how it feels.	2. People like Joanne often behave the way they do because they already feel bad about themselves. What good would it do to contribute to that feeling?
3. I wouldn't want to get involved with her, so I'd just ignore her.	3. Isn't ignoring her actually the same as lying? Is that what you want to do?
4. If I didn't give Joanne her book bag, I'd be as bad as she was.	4. But wouldn't you be encouraging her to keep on behaving badly if you didn't take this opportunity to punish her?

5. Maybe if I'm nice to her, she'll change.

5. What if you tried being nice to her for a while and she didn't change? *Then* would you start treating her like she treats everyone else? Why or why not?

Supplementary Exercise

How are the following three teachings similar? How are they dissimilar? You may wish to keep secret the respective sources of these three passages until the conclusion of the discussion.

1. When you encounter your enemy's ox or donkey wandering, you must take it back to him.
   When you see the donkey of your enemy lying under its burden and would refrain from raising it, you must nevertheless raise it with him.
   Exodus 23:4,5

2. You have heard it said, "Love your neighbor, and hate your enemy, but I say to you: Love your enemies, bless them that curse you, do good to them that hate you, and pray for them that despitefully use you and persecute you."
   Matthew 5:44

3. If someone foolishly does me wrong, I will return to him the protection of my ungrudging love; the more evil comes from him, the more good shall go from me.
   Buddha Gautama

Additional Sources

From the Bible

1. Don't seek revenge or bear a grudge against one of your people, but rather, love your neighbor as yourself.
   Leviticus 19:18

1. לא תקם ולא תטר את בני עמך ואהבת לרעך כמוך (ויקרא, יט, יח).

2. Don't say, "I'll treat him as badly as he treated me"; trust God and He will save you.
   Proverbs 20:22

2. אל תאמר אשלמה רע קווה להי וישע לך (משלי כ׳:כב).

3. Don't be gladdened by your enemies' downfall, nor rejoice when they stumble.

Proverbs 24:17

3. בנפול אויביך אל תשמח ובכשלו אל יגל לבך (משלי כד:יז).

4. If your enemy is hungry, feed him, and if he's thirsty, give him a drink of water.

Proverbs 25:21

4. אם רעב שונאך האכילהו לחם ואם צמא השקהו מים (משלי כה:כא).

From Rabbinic Literature

1. "Don't seek revenge or bear a grudge against one of your people." If in the process of cutting some meat the knife slips and you cut your hand, should the hand holding the knife be cut in revenge?

J. Nedarim, 9:3

1. לא תקם ולא תטר את בני עמך: היך עבידי הוה, מקטע קופד ומחט סכינא לידוי -- תחזור ותמחי לידיה? (ירושי נדרים ט:ג).

2. Concerning those who are insulted but do not insult others [in revenge], who hear themselves reproached without replying, who do [God's will] out of love and rejoice in their sufferings, Scripture says: But they who love Him will be as the sun when it goes forth in its might (Judges 5:31).

Yoma 23a

2. הנעלבין ואינן עולבין, שומעין חרפתן ואינן משיבין, עושין מאהבה ושמחין ביסורין -- עליהן הכתוב אומר: "ואוהבין כצאת השמש בגבורתו", לעולם דנקיט ליה בליביה (יומא כ"ג: א').

3. And Rabah said: Those who show forbearance will be shown forbearance for their sins, as when one tries to make up with another and they are reconciled.

Yoma 23a

3. והאמר רבא: כל המעביר על מדותיו מעבירין לו על כל פשעיו דמפייסו ליה ומפייס (יומא כ"ג:א').

4. Ben Azzai says: "This is the story of humanity ... (who were created in the image of God)." This is a very important principle of the Torah. Rabbi Akiba says, "(Don't seek revenge and don't bear a grudge) ... but rather, love your neighbor as one like yourself." This is a very important principle of the Torah. Thus one should not say, "Since I've been humiliated let someone else be humiliated with me; since I've been hurt let someone else be hurt with me. Rav Tanchuma says: If you act like this, be aware of who you are humiliating: one who was "created in the image of God."

Bereshit Rabbah 24:7

.4 בן עזאי אומר: ״זה ספר תולדות אדם...(בדמות אלוהים עשה אותו)״ - זה כלל גדול בתורה. רבי עקיבא אומר: ״(לא תקם ולא תטר)...ואהבת לרעך כמוך״ -- זה כלל גדול בתורה. שלא תאמר הואיל ונתבזיתי יתבזה חברי עמי הואיל ונתקללתי יתקלל חברי עמי. א״ר תנחומא: אם עשית כן דע למי אתה מבזה - ״בדמות אלהים עשה אותו״ (בראשית רבה כ״ד:ז).

5. "Don't seek revenge": What does seeking revenge entail? Person A says: Lend me your sickle. Person B says: I won't lend it to you. The next day Person B says: Lend me your shovel. Person A says: I won't lend it to you just as you didn't lend me your sickle. This is what "don't seek revenge" means.

"Don't bear a grudge": What does bearing a grudge entail? Person A says: Lend me your shovel. Person B refuses to lend it. The next day Person B says: Lend me your sickle. Person A says: Here it is. I'm not like you — you didn't lend me your shovel. This is what "don't bear a grudge" means.

Sifre 44

.5 ״לא תקם״: עד היכן הוא כוחה של נקימה? א״ל: השאילני מגלך - ולא השאילו. למחר א״ל: השאילני קרדומך, א״ל: איני משאילך כשם שלא השאלת לי מגלך -- לכך נאמר ״לא תקם״;
״לא תטר״: עד היכן כחה של נטירה? א״ל: השאילני קרדומך - ולא השאילו. למחר א״ל: השאילני מגלך- א״ל : הא לך; איני כמותך שלא השאלת לי קרדומך -- לכך נאמר ״לא תטר״ (ספרא מ״ד).

From the *Mishneh Torah*

He who takes revenge violates a transgression, for it is written: "You shall take no revenge." (Leviticus 19:18) And although this offense is not punishable with lashes, it stems nevertheless from an exceedingly bad disposition. One should rather be forebearing with regard to all worldly things which, in the opinion of the wise, are sheer vanity and nothingness; they are not worthy of vengeance.

Ethical Ideas 7:7

הלכות דעות, פרק ז׳׳, יחידות ז׳ ח׳

הנוקם מחברו עובר בלא תעשה, שנאמר: לא תקם (ויקרא יט, יח). ואף על פי שאינו לוקה עליו דעה רעה היא עד מאוד; אלא ראוי לו לאדם להיות מעביר על מדותיו על כל דברי העולם, שהכל אצל המבינים דברי הבל והבאי ואינם כדאי לנקם עליהם. כיצד היא הנקימה? אמר לו חברו: השאילני קרדומך; אמר לו: איני משאילך. למחר נצרך לשאול ממנו. אמר לו: השאילני קרדומך; אמר לו: איני משאילך כדרך שלא השאלתני כששאלתי ממך -- הרי זה נוקם; אלא כשיבא לו לשאול, יתן לו בלב שלם ולא יגמל לו כאשר גמלו.

So too, whoever bears a grudge against a fellow Israelite violates a prohibition, for it is written: "You shall not bear a grudge" (Leviticus 19:18). What is meant by bearing a grudge? A said to B: "Rent this house to me," or: "Lend me this ox." B refused. After some time, B comes to A to borrow or hire something. A replies: "Here it is; I am lending it to you; I am not like you; I will not treat you as you treated me." Whoever acts like this transgresses the command: "You shall not bear a grudge." One should blot the thing out of his mind and not cherish a grudge. For as long as he cherishes a resentment and keeps recalling it, he may come to avenge himself. For this reason, the Torah objects to bearing a grudge, that one may obliterate the wrong from his mind and remember it no more. This is the right way of behavior, whereby civilization and social intercourse are made possible.

Ethical Ideas 7:8

וכן כל הנוטר לאחד מישראל עובר בלא-תעשה. שנאמר: ולא תטר את בני עמך (שם); כיצד היא הנטירה? ראובן שאמר לשמעון: השכר לי בית זה, או השאילני שור זה; ולא רצה שמעון. לימים בא שמעון לראובן לשאול ממנו או לשכר ממנו ואמר לו ראובן: הא לך, הריני משאילך ואיני כמותך. ולא אשלם לך כמעשיך -- העושה כזה עובר ב׳׳לא תטר׳׳; אלא ימחה הדבר מלבו ולא יטרנו, שכל זמן שהוא נוטר את הדבר וזוכרו שמא יבוא לו לנקם. לפיכך הקפידה תורה על הנטירה עד שימחה העוון מליבו

ולא יזכרנו כלל. וזו היא הדעה הנכונה שאפשר שיתקיים בה ישוב הארץ ומשאם ומתנם של בני אדם זה עם זה.

From Malbim's Commentary

Vengeance implies an overt act ... a grudge is in the heart.

Ha-Torah V'Mitzvot
(Leviticus 19:18)

מפירוש מלביים, ״התורה והמצוות״
ויקרא יט:יח:
הנקמה היא בפועל...ונטירה היא בלב.

Further References

1. "Shmuel HaNagid" in *Ivrit Chayah: Modern Hebrew* by Harry Blumberg and Mordecai H. Lewittes. New York: Hebrew Publishing Co., 1946, 232.
2. Buber, Martin. *Hasidism and Modern Man*. New York: Harper Textbooks, 1958, 240. (R. Schmelke of Nikolsburg's comment on revenge)
3. Film: "The Boy Who Liked Deer." "Learning to be Human Series," #5E0961, available from the University of Minnesota Audio-Visual Library, 3300 University Ave. S.E., Minneapolis, Minnesota 55414.

6th Grade – 9th Grade

UNIT IX — Justice and Mercy

מדת הדין ומדת הרחמים

1. Introduction for the Teacher
2. Dilemma Story
3. Suggested Procedure and Cue Sheet
4. Supplementary Exercise
5. Additional Sources

About This Unit

Rabbinic sources often speak of two thrones in heaven, one of *din* (law) and the other of *rachamim* (compassion). In this unit your students will consider whether both of these are really necessary. Might one of the two actually be sufficient?

In the course of discussing this unit's dilemma, you will note how Stage 2 thinkers reason out the problem in terms of fair self-interest. Stage 3 thinkers will emphasize the importance of personal loyalty and friendship, while Stage 4 thinkers will seek to defend the interests of the group as a whole, asserting the primacy of loyalty to one's group over any intervening personal loyalties.

Introduction for The Teacher

"Justice so moves that only those who suffer learn ..."
Agamemnon

Numbers 12:3 informs us that Moses was the humblest person who ever lived. The text apparently includes this fact to explain how it was possible for Miriam and Aaron to scandalize their brother without raising his ire (Numbers 12:1-2). The taunts end only when God intervenes on Moses' behalf, singling out Miriam for harsh punishment (Numbers 12:4-10). The narrative goes on to tell how Moses seeks to undo this punishment, at which point God loses patience with Moses' tolerance, rejecting his intercession with a classically formed legal argument against pardoning Miriam. What is the moral principle underlying God's rejection of Moses' intercession? *Sifra* makes this observation: "Why then weren't you afraid to challenge my servant, [to challenge] Moses?" (Numbers

12:9) ... This case is like the case of a ruler who has a representative in a certain province whom residents of that province challenge. The king would say to them, "You haven't challenged my servant — you have challenged me ..." (See this unit's Supplementary Exercise for the complete quotation.).

Sifra suggests that from God's perspective the personal dimension of the conflict between Moses, Miriam and Aaron is secondary. What is primary is the assertion of God's just authority to delegate power as God sees fit. Neither Aaron's regret nor Moses' forgiveness speak to this aspect of the conflict; God's authority must be publicly reestablished, and this entails the meting out of punishment.

This unit's dilemma story is based on Numbers 12:1-16 and revolves around the issues raised in *Sifra*: What is the relationship between rightful authority, personal sentiments and loyalties, law and order?

Dilemma Story

Michelle was the captain of the Northside All-Stars basketball team. For many years the team's assistant captains, Andrea and Miriam, had been Michelle's best friends, but lately that had seemed to change. Andrea and Miriam thought that Michelle had gotten awfully conceited and bossy since becoming team captain, and that she didn't fairly share her authority with them.

The afternoon of the big Northside-Southside game, Miriam hit upon a plan to put Michelle in her place. Miriam went from team member to team member telling them not to listen to any of Michelle's directions during the game, but to follow any directions she, Miriam, or Andrea gave. Miriam was in the locker room explaining her plan to one of the team members when Mrs. Davids, the coach, came in. Mrs. Davids caught enough of the conversation to understand what Miriam was up to. When Miriam turned around to see who had come in, Mrs. Davids said, "Miriam, you don't deserve to be an assistant captain. Your job is to help keep the team together and enthusiastic and it looks like you're doing just the opposite!" She stopped a moment and then added, "You'll sit out today's game."

When Andrea came into the locker room a few minutes later, she found Miriam sitting all alone and crying. Miriam told Andrea what had happened, that she was very sorry for what she'd done and that she really wanted to play that afternoon.

Andrea went directly to Michelle, told her everything, and asked her to talk to the coach about letting Miriam play. Andrea said that if Michelle asked, there was a chance the coach would change her mind. Though they hadn't been getting along very well lately, Michelle still considered Miriam one of her best friends. Michelle felt very sorry for Miriam. She also thought that she should be loyal to her old friend, and so she agreed to talk to Mrs. Davids about letting Miriam play.

By the time Michelle found the coach, the team was already suiting up. When she asked if Miriam could play, Mrs. Davids replied, "This team has a captain — you, and you're a good one. The team also has a system by which it operates and it was wrong of Miriam to try and mess that system up. Miriam needs to understand that what happened isn't just between you two — it affects the whole team."

Michelle responded, "I forgive Miriam. I think she understands now that what she did was wrong, and she's really sorry about it. Please let her play."

To this Mrs. Davids replied, "I'm not so sure that it's a matter of her being sorry or of you forgiving her ... but I tell you what. You're the captain. I'll leave it up to you.

What do you think? Should Miriam have to sit out the game? Why or why not?

Suggested Procedure

1. Read the dilemma story with the class.
2. Poll the class on the dilemma question.
3. Have each student explain his or her response to the dilemma question, alternating between students who differ as to the proper solution to the dilemma.
4. You may wish to use the following questions to stimulate discussion and raise issues which the students may otherwise overlook:
   a. Should the fact that Miriam is one of Michelle's best friends affect her decision?
   b. What do you consider worse: Miriam's personal disloyalty to Andrea or the possible consequences of her actions for the team as a whole?
   c. What is the responsibility and proper course of action for the rest of the team members in this situation?
5. Do the supplementary exercise.

Cue Sheet

Below, on the left, are some points your students might bring up in the course of discussing this unit's dilemma. On the right you will find some suggested responses to these comments. These critical responses are designed to help focus discussion on possible weaknesses or contradictions in the reasoning which led to the initial comment. It is most often preferable that these sorts of responses come from other classmates, but if such challenges are not forthcoming, you yourself should provide them.

Student Statements	Possible Teacher Response
1. Loyalty to friends comes first.	1. Won't not punishing Miriam encourage other players who are unhappy about one thing or another to try to disrupt the team? Pretty soon the whole team could be a mess.
2. If Miriam weren't punished, it would ruin the team's morale.	2. Does Miriam have a *right* to play after doing what she did?
3. If Miriam is a very good player, she should play. Why make it more difficult for the rest of the team by benching one of the best players?	3. It's in everybody's self-interest that rules are impartially enforced — that's part of what is meant by teamwork.
4. Miriam should be punished to teach her a lesson — so that she doesn't do something similar in the future.	4. Miriam seems genuinely sorry. What more can she do?
5. Miriam should be treated as she tried to treat Michelle.	5. Then what would be the difference between Miriam and those who gave her "some of their own medicine?"

Supplementary Exercise

This unit's dilemma story was adapted from Numbers 12:1-16. You may wish to examine this passage with your class in connection with the following comment from *Sifra loc. cit.*

"Why then weren't they afraid ..." (Numbers 12:8): It says, "to challenge my servant, (to challenge) Moses" because "you speak against Me when you speak against My servant Moses." This case is like the case of a ruler who has a representative in a certain province whom the residents of that province challenge. The king would say to them, "You haven't challenged my representative — you have challenged me." And if you claim you didn't realize who he was, that's even worse!"

How does *Sifra's* comment relate to this unit's dilemma story?

Additional Sources

From Rabbinic Literature

1. Rabbi Eleazar, the son of Rabbi Yose the Galilean says: It is forbidden to strike a deal on a case which should be decided by a court. Anyone who strikes a deal is a sinner ... Rather, one should let the chips fall where they may [lit.: let the law pierce the mountain] ... Indeed, Moses used to say, "let the chips fall where they may," but Aaron loved and pursued peace; he was a peacemaker, as it says: He taught a trustworthy Torah. He was never dishonest. He walked with Me in peace and equity, keeping many from falling away (Malachi 2:6).

Sanhedrin 6b

1. ר״א בנו של רבי יוסי הגלילי אומר אסור לבצוע וכל הבוצע ה״ז חוטא... אלא יקוב הדין את ההר... וכן משה היה אומר יקוב הדין את ההר אבל אהרון אוהב שלום ורודף שלום ומשיב שלום בין אדם לחברו, שנאמר תורת אמת היתה בפיהו ועוולה לא נמצא בשפתין; בשלום ובמישור הלך אתי ורבים השיב מעוון (סנהדרין ו׳:ב׳).

2. Rabbi Shimon B. Lakish says: One who is compassionate when hardheartedness is called for will end up being hardhearted when compassion is called for ... Rabanan said that whoever is compassionate when hardheartedness is called for, *midat ha-din* (justice) will eventually catch up with him ...

Kohelet Rabbah 7

2. רשב״ל אומר כל מי שנעשה רחמן במקום אכזרי סוף שנעשה אכזרי במקום רחמן... ורבנן אמרין כל מי שנעשה רחמן במקום אכזרי סוף שמדת הדין פוגעת בו... (קוהלת רבה ז׳).

6th Grade - 9th Grade

UNIT X — Law and Order

הטוב והישר

1. Introduction for the Teacher
2. Dilemma Story
3. Suggested Procedure and Cue Sheet
4. Supplementary Exercise
5. Additional Sources

About This Unit

In this unit your students will explore the question: Is one justified in disobeying a law which, in a given case, appears to be dysfunctional? For instance, need one stop at a red light in the middle of the night at a totally deserted intersection?

Students who primarily reason at Stage 3 and below will tend to approach this problem from a perspective which is basically personal: What are the consequences *to me* of obeying (or disobeying) the rule in question? Students reasoning at Stage 4 or above, on the other hand, will begin to express concern for the *social* consequences of an action: What would happen if everyone disobeyed this rule?

Introduction for the Teacher

"Every law has its rationale, but the rationale is not sovereign over the law, and is not necessarily a condition for its authority. And the rationale itself sometimes seems apparent and sometimes not, or may not even be discernable at all. Thus it is that in most cases a person may not invoke a rationale to undermine the law, and that the benefit gained by knowing the rationale shall not be paid for by a disparagement of the law."

From *Talmudic Law and the Modern State*, by Moshe Silberg (New York: Burning Bush Press, 1973), p. 55.

In his *Statesman*, Plato discusses the great difficulty of devising rules that can both meet the needs of the community and also accurately allot to each individual his or her due. Plato states that "Law can never issue an injunction binding on all which really embodies what is best for each; it cannot prescribe with perfect accuracy what is good and right for each member of the community at any one time. The differences of human personality, the variety of men's activities, and the inevitable unsettlement attending all human experience make it impossible for any art whatsoever to issue unqualified rules holding good on all questions at all times."[1]

Plato's understanding of law suggests that the ideal of "a government of laws and not of men" is a double-edged sword, for though law can help to protect the community from the arbitrary self-interest of individuals, it does so by establishing an abstract arbitrariness of its own. This being the case, Plato concludes that a legal system can only function if those who are subject to it are willing to tolerate its minimal dysfunction. A legislator can do no better than design laws "for the generality of his subjects under average circumstances. Thus he will legislate for all individual citizens, but it will be by what may be called a 'bulk' method rather than an individual treatment, and this method of 'bulk' prescription will be followed by him whether he makes a written code of law or refrains from issuing such a code, preferring to legislate by using unwritten ancestral customs."[2]

Plato considers it inevitable that at times a gap will appear between the "abstract average" of law and the actual circumstances surrounding a particular individual's actions. In such cases a wedge is driven between a law and its rationale. Consider, for example, the laws concerning traffic lights. Stopping at red lights is one of the more universal fixtures of modern legislation, and yet we all know of exceptions to the rule. Most people would agree that it would be absurd to require emergency vehicles to stop at red lights. Is it then no less absurd to require someone to stop at a red light at a clearly deserted intersection at three in the morning? The purpose of the red light is to regulate traffic. If there is no traffic, what is the status of the law?

In this unit's dilemma we consider the question: if the rationale for a given rule does not appear to apply, may one conclude that the rule itself likewise does not apply?

Dilemma Story

At certain times during the day, a teacher's aide runs a little shop at Joel's school where students can buy notebooks, pencils and snacks. One morning, right before his first period class, Joel realized that he had left his new notebook at home. Joel's teacher had told everyone to bring a new notebook that day for a project they would be beginning during first period. Joel was a little behind in his first period class, so he wanted to get started on the new project as soon as possible. Since the shop that sold school supplies happened to be open before first period, Joel decided to buy another notebook.

By the time Joel got to the shop there were already several students waiting to buy something. Joel got in line and waited patiently, but just as his turn came up, the teacher's aide was called away. Several minutes passed. Finally the bell rang, and the aide had not yet returned.

Joel thought to himself that it didn't make much sense for him to have waited all the time without getting a notebook. He figured the logical thing to do was to pay his money, make his own change and take a notebook. The only problem was that no one except the teacher's aide was allowed to touch the money box or the supplies.

While Joel was standing there trying to decide what to do, Ann and Gary came by. Joel told them what had happened and each of them told him what they thought he should do.

Ann said that if someone saw Joel taking something from the shop, he could get into trouble even if he wasn't stealing, because the rule is that students can't even *touch* the stuff in the shop. And besides, she said, if rules are going to have any effect, they have to apply to everyone. If Joel didn't follow the rules, why should anyone else? Ann concluded that if she were Joel, she'd do without the notebook rather than break the rules.

Gary disagreed. He felt that the point of the rule was to keep people from stealing and that since Joel wasn't stealing, the rule didn't apply. Gary thought that the right thing to do in this case was for Joel to wait on himself. He figured that the rule was there to make sure that snacks and school supplies would be available for everyone, so it didn't make any sense to let the rule keep Joel from getting a notebook.

What do you think Joel should do? Why?

Suggested Procedure

1. Read the dilemma story with the class.
2. Poll the class on the dilemma question.
3. Have each student explain his or her response to the dilemma question, alternating between students who differ as to the proper solution to the dilemma.
4. You may wish to use the following questions to stimulate discussion and raise issues which the students may otherwise overlook:
   a. Do you think it is a good idea to punish people who break rules? Why or why not? If you *do* think it is a good idea, how

does one determine what constitutes an appropriate punishment for a given violation?

b. Do you think that persons who are responsible for enforcing rules should take a violator's intentions into account when considering whether that person should be punished for the violation?
c. Do you think that the intent of a given law should be taken into account when considering whether someone who has violated it should be punished?
d. If Joel got permission from his first hour teacher to take a notebook, would you then agree that it was all right for him to do so?

5. Do the supplementary exercise.

Cue Sheet

Below, on the left, are some points your students might bring up in the course of discussing this unit's dilemma. On the right you'll find some suggested responses to these comments. These critical responses are designed to help focus discussion on possible weaknesses or contradictions in the reasoning which led to the initial comment. It is most often preferable that these sorts of responses come from other classmates, but if such challenges are not forthcoming you yourself should provide them.

Student Statements	Possible Teacher Response
1. I'd get someone to be my witness that I wasn't stealing anything.	1. Your intentions are irrelevant. Rules deal with actions, not intentions, and your actions are against the rules.
2. It doesn't make any sense to follow rules that obviously don't apply to you or to your situation.	2. Rules are made with the best interests of the *group* in mind, not necessarily the interests of individuals. What's the sense of having rules at all if each individual reserves the right to decide which ones he or she will obey?

3. If I suspected that the teacher would act unreasonably if I came without a notebook, I'd go ahead and take one — to protect myself. I think I have that right.

3. What if it was your best friend who needed the notebook? Assuming that your friend has the same right that you do to self-protection, would you break the rule for her/his sake? What if it were likely that you'd be punished for it? What if it was for a stranger? What if the other person probably wouldn't do the same thing for you?

4. It all depends on which would get me in more trouble — coming to class without a notebook, or taking a notebook without permission.

4. Does that mean that if there were no such thing as punishment, you'd have no way of knowing what's right and what's wrong?

5. A rule's a rule and should be obeyed.

5. Do you think the Maccabees were wrong to refuse to obey Antiochus' rules? If not, what's the difference?

Supplementary Exercise

In the following exercise the students will explore how other teen-agers and adults in their community reason about moral problems. This exercise can deal with your community's reserved handicapped parking law or with some analogous regulation. A suggested procedure is as follows:

1. Briefly discuss with your class the question at the top of the following Survey Sheet.
2. Explain to your students that they are going to survey others in the community concerning this same question.
3. Go over the paragraph at the top of the Survey Sheet with your students. They should clearly understand:
   a. What they are trying to find out: What do people think of non-handicapped drivers parking in a space which is reserved for handicapped drivers if there's virtually no chance of a handicapped driver actually needing that space?
   b. How to find that out:
      1) by finding a parking lot with reserved handicapped parking

2) by getting the permission of the store manager to survey people using that lot
3) by complying with the manager's instructions
4) by being courteous
5) by taking short, specific notes

4. Arrange for students to work in pairs so that they have someone with whom they can immediately discuss their findings.
5. Set a date for comparison and discussion of survey results.
6. Questions for the discussion:
   a. What was the most common response?
   b. What was the most common rationale?
   c. Did two people who disagreed on *what* to do agree on *why* to do it?
   d. How did the survey results compare with the class' own discussion of the dilemma?
   e. Did certain groups of people give certain types of answers?

SURVEY SHEET

Hello, My name is ________. I am a student at __________. I am doing a survey as part of a class project. Could I please ask you my survey question? (If "yes"): Do you think that it would be all right to park in a "*Handicapped Only*" space in this parking lot if there were only one or two other cars in the lot and it was a very cold night in January? Why? Why not? What if all the other places were already taken?

	Is all right	Isn't all right	Why
1.			
2.			
3.			
4.			
5.			
6.			
7.			
8.			
9.			
10.			
11.			
12.			
13.			

Additional Sources:

From Rabbinic Literature

1. Rabbi Yitzchak said: Why weren't the rationales of the [*mitzvot* in the] Torah revealed? Take a look! In the two texts where their rationales are given one of the greatest stumbled. It is written "He must not get more and more wives" (Deuteronomy 17:17). Solomon said, "I'll have more and more and I won't go astray," and yet it is written, "In Solomon's old age his wives bent his heart" (I Kings 11:4). It is also written, "He must not get more and more horses" (Deuteronomy 17:16). Solomon said, "I'll get more and more and I won't send back ....", and yet it is written, "A chariot was exported from Egypt..." (I Kings 10:29).

Sanhedrin 21b

1. אמר ר׳ יצחק מה לא נתגלה טעמי תורה שהרי שתי מקראות נתגלו טעמן נכשל בהן גדול עולם כתיב לא ירבה לו נשים אמר שלמה אני ארבה דלא אסור וכתיב ויהי לעת זקנת שלמה נשיו הטו את לבבו וכתיב לא ירבה לו סוסים ואמר שלמה אני ארבה ולא אשיב וכתיב ותצא מרכבה ממצרים...

סנהדרין כא:ב

2. What is a pious fool? A man who sees a woman drowning in the river and says, "It would be bad manners on my part to gaze upon her and save her..." (*Tosephot*: He sees a baby drowning [lit.: bubbling] in a river and says, "I'll save him after I've taken off my *tefillin*." By the time he has gotten off his *tefillin*, he'll have caused the child's death.)

Sotah 21b

2. הכי דמי חסיד שוטה כגון דקא טבעה איתתא בנהרא ואמר לאו אורח ארעא לאיסתכולי בה ואצולה...

(תוספות: ראה תינוק מבעבע בנהר אמר לכשאחלוץ תפילין אצילנו עד כשהוא חולץ תפילין הוציא זה את נפשו).

סוטה כא:ב

Mekor Hesed on *Sefer Hasidim* 510:

Here and elsewhere our teacher offered possible rationales for certain texts, but this is not meant to suggest that the rationale is the basis and the motive for the *mitzvah* to the extent that if the rationale no longer applied the *mitzvah* would also not apply ... As it is explained in the Jerusalem Talmud (*Peah* 84:2): It has been taught in the name of Rabbi Shimon [bar Yochai] that there are five reasons why one must only give *Peah* from the edges of one's field, (1) . . . (2) . . . (3) . . . (4) . . . and (5) *because the Torah said,* "You must not reap all the way to the edge of your field." My point is that Rabbi Shimon bar Yochai, a master of the Torah's mysteries, though able to offer numerous logical rationales for *mitzvot* and the details of their *halachot* nevertheless emphasizes that, in the end, all the rationales and motives come down to this: the Torah said it.

מקור חסד לספר חסידים תקי״י:

הנה רבינו כאן ובכמה מקומות דרש טעמי דקרא אבל אין הכוונה שהטעם שנאמר הוא יסוד וסיבת המצווה עד כי בהתבטלות הטעם תתבטל המצווה... ומבואר בירושלמי פאה פ״ד ה״ב: תני בשם ר׳ שמעון מפני חמישה דברים לא יתן אדם פאה אלא בסוף שדהו מפני.... מפני... מפני.... מפני... ומפני שאמרה תורה לא תכלה פאת שדך כו׳, שר״ל ר׳ שמעון בן יוחאי בעל רזי תורה הוא הדורש בכ״מ טעמים הגיוניים למצות ולפרטי הלכותיהן אבל הדגיש כי סוף כל הטעמים והנימוקים היא מפני שאמרה תורה.

7th Grade – 10th Grade

UNIT XI — Social Contract

ברית

1. Introduction for the Teacher
2. Dilemma Story
3. Suggested Procedure and Cue Sheet
4. Additional Material on Social Contract and Brit and Supplementary Exercise
5. Additional Sources

About This Unit

For a group to maintain itself, it must achieve a certain degree of cooperation and cohesion. Very little can be accomplished by a group which is in non-cooperative disarray. But is there a point where a legitimate concern for cohesion ends and illegitimate peer pressure begins? If so, what role should the individual group member play in defining the degree to which his or her cooperation can be the result of either one's *preferences* or *principles*. Should this distinction play any role in determining the degree to which one should cooperate, or the appropriateness of coercing participation in a given group activity? These are the sorts of questions raised by this unit's dilemma.

Introduction for the Teacher

Human beings pursue goals both in groups and as individuals. If a group is to prosper, its members must agree sometimes to yield a portion of their self-interest toward the pursuit of the goals of the group as a whole. For instance, you may find stopping at traffic lights bothersome and inconvenient, but society compels you to pursue the interests of the group by observing the traffic laws.

That people, more or less successfully, organize themselves into a great variety of groups suggests that we most often find it possible to identify or harmonize our individual goals with the goals of the groups in which we participate. Mahatma Gandhi commented in this regard: "We have learned to strike the mean between individual freedom and social restraint. Willing submission to social restraint for the sake of the well-being of the whole society enriches both the individual and the society of which one is a member."[1]

In this unit we explore how individuals respond to demands placed upon them by the groups of which they are members. Do individual and group interests always coincide? If not, which takes precedence? What if the individual sees the conflict as concerning an issue of principle, rather than of simple self-interest?

The term "social contract" was popularized by Jean Jacques Rousseau as the title and topic of one of his philosohical works, but the idea for which it stands is an ancient one. The "social contract" refers to a process whereby we as individuals give a group some degree of authority to regulate our behavior in return for the order and mutual benefit that such regulation is expected to bring. This model of society, which underlies the dilemma story that follows, is subsumed among Jewish value concepts under the category of *brit* (covenant). *Brit*, however, is more than simply a synonym for "social contract." The covenant at Sinai is both horizontal and vertical in the sense that the same instrument that binds the people to one another also binds them to God. A *brit* is not only a social contract between human beings, but, to use Franz Rosenzweig's term, exists in the context of "theo-human reality." This is why the Bible speaks of social misconduct as sin. God, as Rabbi Akiba points out, is the constant third party in every human interaction.

The following supplementary information is meant as an aid for students to expand the social contract theme of this unit's dilemma to the full dimensions of *brit*.

For the Student

A *brit* is an agreement by two or more parties to regulate their relationships with one another on the basis of certain agreed upon obligations. Many people who have studied the way human beings organize themselves into groups have concluded that some type of *brit* is the basis for all forms of human society. Modern scholars call these basic *britot* the "social contract." In fact, both the Hebrew word *brit* and the Latin based term "contract" come from roots which mean "bringing together."

What then does it mean to be *ba'ale brit*: parties to a *brit*? The minimum commitment of a *brit* is usually an agreement not to use violence against one another. It is clear that any group whose members do not share such a commitment is not likely to last long. In addition to this commitment to non-violence, most groups are organized around the pursuit of certain group goals. Cities, for instance, are organized for the purpose of providing their residents with services which can be obtained more effectively as a group than as individuals: education, protection from crime and fire, etc.

The Torah describes how Abraham and his descendants came to believe that the one and only God sought to form *brit* relationships with human beings. Here, as is also the case with purely human *britot*, the basic purpose of the *brit* is to allow God and human beings to exist together in harmony, without recourse to violence. Thus, we read that after Noah's generation was destroyed by the flood, God made a *brit* with all living things, to draw the creatures of the earth into a relationship which would not end in the kind of destruction that had just occurred (Genesis 9:12-17).

What is the connection between a *brit* that human beings have with one another and a *brit* between human beings and God? Jewish tradition teaches that these two forms of *brit* are ultimately one and the same. This is why doing wrong to another human being is a sin against God. Rabbi Akiva (50-135 C.E.) explained it this way, based on the following text from Torah:

"If someone sins by cheating God through false dealings with a neighbor ..." (Leviticus 5:21).

Rabbi Akiva says: "What does the Torah mean by 'cheating God?'" Loans and business transactions are only made with witnesses and documents, and so cheating entails contradicting witnesses and documents. But someone who gives something to another for safe keeping doesn't want anyone else to know about it except for the Third who is among them. Therefore, when he contradicts, he contradicts the Third who is among them" (Rashi *loc. cit.* based on *Sifra*).

Dilemma Story

Mike is a member of a certain youth group. Being a member of this group is important to Mike, because lots of his friends are also members. Additionally, he enjoys and benefits from many of the group's activities.

In November, most of the group's members decide that they would like to take a trip to Chicago during the winter break. The group's president decides that because time is short and costs for the trip would be quite high, *all* group members should help raise money, whether they plan to go or not. The majority of the group choose a candy sale as the way to raise the necessary money.

Mike is not interested in going on the trip. In fact, he feels that such trips are a waste of time and a poor use of the money they might raise. Mike also finds selling candy slightly embarrassing. All in all, there are many other ways he would rather spend his time.

Eddie is also a member of the group. Mike meets Eddie in the school cafeteria the day after the group decided to take the trip. Mike mentions to Eddie that he's not interested in the trip and doesn't want to sell candy. Eddie tells Mike that he shouldn't feel obligated to raise money for a project he doesn't support and suggests that Mike tell this to the group's president. Mike does so at the next meeting. The president replies that it may not seem fair to ask those who don't want to go to support those who do, but the fact is that if all members don't help sell candy, some who want to go may not be able to afford the trip. If this were true, perhaps it would only be fair that no one went. Greg, who had come up with the idea of the trip in the first place, adds that if Mike doesn't want to cooperate with the majority, maybe he shouldn't be in the group.

The president again asks that all group members help raise the money, whether they plan to go on the trip or not.

Question: Should or shouldn't Mike help sell the candy?

Suggested Procedure

1. Read the dilemma story with the class.
2. Poll the class on the dilemma question.
3. Have each student explain his or her response to the dilemma question, alternating between students who differ as to the proper solution to the dilemma.
4. In the course of discussing the question found at the end of this unit's dilemma story, it may be helpful to:
   a. Focus part of the discussion on specific statements made by characters in the story, e.g., "Do you agree with Greg that if Mike doesn't want to cooperate with the majority, maybe he shouldn't be in the group at all?"
   b. Ask if the nature of the specific issue at stake makes a difference (principle vs. interest). For instance, what if you are *shomer Shabbat* (a person who observes Shabbat in the traditional manner) and the candy sale takes place on Shabbat? What if you are asked to sell under false pretenses (e.g., the person asking misleads you regarding the group he/she represents and/or the purpose of the fundraiser)?
   c. Explore the effect that non-cooperation by individuals and minority factions have on a group.
   d. Discuss the difference between majority rule and consensus. What type of group (i.e., its size, purpose, composition) would be most appropriate for each?
5. Read the supplementary article.

Cue Sheet

Below, on the left, are some points your students might bring up in the course of discussing this unit's dilemma. On the right you'll find some suggested responses to these comments. These critical responses are designed to help focus discussion on possible weaknesses or contradictions in the reasoning which led to the initial comment. It is most often preferable that these sorts of responses come from other classmates, but if such challenges are not forthcoming, you yourself should provide them.

Student Statements	Possible Teacher Response
1. It's not fair to make someone raise money for something they're not going to use.	1. Does that include raising money for *tzedakah*?
2. Majority rules. Whatever the majority decides is what everyone should do.	2. What's so special about majorities? Some decisions in Congress must be supported by two thirds of the members. Sometimes a jury must reach a unanimous decision.
3. Mike should sell the candy now and then, maybe, the other group members will agree to do something that Mike really wants to do in the future.	3. What if, in the future, the group turns down all Mike's suggestions of things to do? Should he still continue to cooperate with the others?
4. I wouldn't be a member of a group that made me do things I didn't want to do.	4. Would you be a member of a sports team even if you didn't get to play as much as you'd like?
5. If Mike voted for the president of the group, he's obligated to follow him. Otherwise, he's not.	5. Are you obligated to follow a teacher's directions? Why? (Point out that you are speaking about obligation, not avoidance of punishment.)

Supplementary Exercise

In Rabbi Akiva's explanation of Leviticus 5:21 (see Introduction for the Teacher above), discuss who he means by the "Third" among them — (God).

Additional Sources

From Rabbinic Literature

1. Hillel says: Don't separate yourself from the community.

Pirke Avot 2:5

1. הלל אומר: אל תפרש מן הצבור (אבות ב׳).

2. Samuel said: A person should never make himself an exception to the rule.

Berachot 49b

2. אמר שמואל: לעולם אל יוציא אדם את עצמו מן הכלל (ברכות מ״ט:ב).

3. Rabbi Shimon b. Yochai taught: This is like some people who were sitting in a boat. One of them picked up a drill and started to drill a hole underneath himself. The other said to him: "What do you think you're doing?" He said: "What do *you* care? Aren't I drilling under my own place?"

Leviticus Rabbah 4:6

3. שנה רשב״י: משל לבני אדם שהיו יושבין בספינה. נטל אחד מהן מקדח והתחיל קודח תחתיו. אמרו לו חבריו: מה אתה יושב ועושה? אמר להם: מה איכפת לכם? לא תחתי אני קודח? (ויקרא ר׳, ד:ו).

4. All of Israel is responsible for each other. To what can they be compared? To a boat which springs a leak in one of its compartments. They don't say, "One compartment of the boat has sprung a leak," but rather, "the whole boat has sprung a leak."

Tana D. Eliahu Rabbah II

4. כל ישראל ערבים זה בזה. למה הם דומים? לספינה שנקרע בה בית אחד. אין אומרים: נקרע בית אחד בספינה, אלא נקרעה כל הספינה כלה (תדא״ר ב׳).

5. A person should suffer along with the community, for thus we find that Moses our Teacher suffered along with the community,

as it says, "Moses' hands became heavy so they took a stone and put it under him and he sat upon it" (Exodus 17). Didn't Moses have a pillow or cushion upon which he could sit? But Moses looked at it this way: Since Israel is suffering, I must be with them in their suffering. Thus, everyone who shares in the suffering of the community gains the right to share in the community's consolation.

Ta'anit II

5. יצער אדם עם הציבור, שכן מצינו במשה רבנו שציער עצמו עם הציבור, שנאמר: וידי משה כבדים ויקחו אבן וישימו תחתיו וישב עליה (שמות יז). וכי לא היה לו למשה כר אחת או כסת אחת לישב עליה? אלא כך אמר משה: הואיל וישראל שרויין בצער אף אני אהיה עמהם בצער. וכל המצער עצמו עם הציבור זוכה ורואה בנחמת צבור (תענית יא:א).

6. The world is suspended by (the thread of) self-restraint. R. Elai said: The world would not continue to exist if it weren't for those who restrain themselves in times of discord.

Chulin 99

6. ״יתלה הארץ על בלימה״: אמר ר׳ אלעי: אין העולם מתקיים אלא בשביל מי שבולם את עצמו בשעת מריבה (חולין פ״ט).

Additional Sources

From *Mishnah Torah*

1. Anyone who stands aloof from the community, even though he commits no transgressions but only separates himself from the Jewish people and does not perform *mitzvot* as one of them, nor does he share in their distress nor observe their fasts, but proceeds on his own way, as if he were a non-Jew and not one of the community, such an individual has no share in the world to come.

Laws of Repentance 3:11

1. משנה תורה, הלכות תשובה, פי 3, יחידה 11:

הפורש מדרכי צבור - אף על פי שלא עבר עברות אלא נבדל מדעת ישראל ואינו עושה מצוות בכללן, ולא נכנס בצרתם ולא מתענה בתעניתם, אלא הולך בדרכו כאחד מגויי הארץ וכאילו אינו מהם, אין לו חלק לעולם הבא.

2. An excellent film dealing with the problem of self-interest in conflict with responsibility to a group is:

   "Angel and Big Joe," #7E0960 in the "Learning to be Human Series." Available from the University of Minnesota Audio-visual Library, 3300 University Avenue S.E., Minneapolis, MN 55414.

9th Grade – 12th Grade

UNIT XII — Amos & Amaziah

עמוס ואמציה

1. Introduction for The Teacher
2. Dilemma Story
3. Suggested Procedure and Cue Sheet
4. Supplementary Exercise
5. Additional Sources

About This Unit

Achieving a just social order is the great vision of the prophets. But are there occasions when one must choose *between* justice and order? If so, how does one make the choice? This is the topic of Unit XII.

Students reasoning below Stage 5 will have difficulty understanding how fidelity to moral principles might serve as a rationale for challenging the forces of law and order. A concern for fulfilling one's assigned role in society, or avoidance of punishment and ostracism, will characterise these students' approach to this dilemma. Students reasoning at Stage 5, on the other hand, will tend to view human rights as "inalienable" and law as socially contracted. Such students will have little difficulty appreciating the potential for conflict between the moral principles one might hold and the social order of which one is a part.

Introduction for The Teacher

"Established religious authority, personified by the priesthood ... in order to maintain itself, by virtue of its pact with power, in possession of the particular sphere which the latter had assigned to it, disassociated itself from the claim of the religious principle to be the mover of the whole. That coalition of established power and established authority was faced by the prophet as the man who had neither power nor authority."

On Judaism by Martin Buber (New York: Schocken Books, 1967), p. 197

Time buries all institutions which do not periodically renew themselves through institutional *teshuvah* (repentance). Guiding this *teshuvah* is the central task of a prophet. However, great religious principles cannot long endure outside the sheath of religious institutions. Such institutions were personified during the biblical period by the priesthood.

We are skeptical these days of attributing the motivation for a particular act to prophetic inspiration, yet the process within which the ethically prophetic stand confronts institutional authority continues to operate in our day as it did in the biblical period. In this unit we examine a contemporary parallel to the confrontation of Amos the prophet with Amaziah the priest at the Royal Sanctuary of Bethel, 740 B.C.E. We are concerned with examining the ethical issues involved in acting on one's own perception of justice in confrontation with an authority which claims to represent the highest values of society.

Dilemma Story

A Confrontation in the Synagogue

It is Yom Kippur and you are one of the ushers in the synagogue. The Rabbi has impressed upon you the importance of your role in maintaining the dignity and decorum of the service. You take your role and responsibility very seriously.

The reader of the Haftarah comes to the passage:

> "Isn't *this* the fast I've chosen
> to loose the bonds of wickedness,
> to undo the thongs of the yoke,
> to free the oppressed
> and to break every yoke!
> To share your bread with the hungry,
> bringing the homeless poor into your house ...
>
> Isaiah 58:6,7

An unfamiliar person stands up and calls out: "Didn't you hear what the Haftarah said? We can't continue this service when three quarters of the world's people are hungry and oppressed! I refuse to allow this service to continue until we respond to the message of the Haftarah." A commotion begins among the congregants. Many appear frightened and upset. The Rabbi calmly steps to the microphone and says: "Will the ushers please restore order so the service may continue."

Suggested Procedure

1. Together read the Dilemma story.
2. Discuss the following question: As an usher, which of these three courses of action do you think you should follow and why (force yourself to choose the best of the three):
   a. You should do nothing.
   b. You should openly declare that you think the speaker's point should be considered here and now (and that you therefore refuse to help stop the interruption).
   c. You should politely but firmly proceed to have the person seated or leave the room.
3. If none of the students choose response b, you may wish to read them chapter 7, verses 7-17 of the book of Amos. Explain to the students that in this confrontation with Amaziah the priest, Amos acted very much like the interrupter in this dilemma story. Would they have remained silent or ejected Amos?
4. You may wish to use the following questions to help stimulate and direct the discussion of the dilemma.
   a. If you agree that the "interrupter" (or Amos) was justified in interrupting the service, is there any event or situation you can think of in which their actions would *not* be justified?
   b. Why is there a book of the Bible entitled Amos, but not one entitled Amaziah?
   c. Do you think you would treat the "interrupter" differently if, rather than being a stranger, he/she was:
      1) the most generous giver of *tzedakah* in the congregation
      2) the poorest member of the congregation
      3) the oldest member of the congregation
      4) someone known to be highly knowledgeable in Torah
      5) a highly respected doctor/scientist/professor
      6) a highly influential business executive

Cue Sheet

Below, on the left, are some points your students might bring up in the course of discussing this unit's dilemma. On the right you will find some suggested responses to these comments. These critical responses are designed to help focus discussion on possible weaknesses or contradictions in the reasoning which led to the initial comment. It is most often preferable that these sorts of responses come from other classmates, but if such challenges are not forthcoming, you yourself should provide them.

Student Statements	Possible Teacher Response
1. People come to the synagogue to pray and it is the responsibility of the synagogue staff to help them do so, without interruptions.	1. What if someone became very ill while in the sanctuary? Would it be proper to interrupt the service to aid that person? What if that person became ill in the coatroom / vestibule / lobby? What about in the parking lot? At what point is the person too far away to justify interrupting the service?
2. You can't solve the problem of hunger right now anyway.	2. But doesn't the Haftarah seem to be making exactly the same point — that worship is not effective as long as there is hunger in the world? Therefore, logic would seem to suggest that the ushers stop the reader as well!
3. The Rabbi is in charge. It's up to the Rabbi to decide what is to be done.	3. How exactly *is* a Rabbi "in charge?" From where does a Rabbi's authority come?
4. Most of the people who go to the synagogue on Yom Kippur are phonies, anyway. It might do them some good to hear the man out.	4. What if, instead of occurring on Yom Kippur, this happened on the day that you were celebrating your becoming a Bar/Bat Mitzvah?
5. If you accepted the responsibility of being a good usher, you must do as the Rabbi asks.	5. Can you be held to a commitment made under normal circumstances if unforeseen, extraordinary circumstances arise?

Supplementary Exercise

The passage below is taken from "Billy Budd," a three act play by Louis O.Coxe and Robert Chapman. The play is an adaptation of

Herman Melville's novel *Billy Budd, Foretopman*. The plot, in brief, is as follows: Billy Budd, a good and endearing young sailor, is falsely accused of conspiring to mutiny by Claggart, a bitter and jealous petty officer. Billy, in speechless disbelief, strikes Claggart, killing him. By killing a superior officer, Billy, ironically enough, has committed a sort of mutiny, for which the penalty is death. A court-martial is held at which several of the participants claim that regardless of the dictates of law, their consciences do not allow them to execute one like Billy, In other words, they wish to defend Billy by dint of a "higher law." The excerpt provided comes at this point in the trial. Captain Vere, though sympathetic with the call for clemency, nevertheless maintains that it is the responsibility of those vested with authority to exercise that authority in a uniform and impartial manner, even, if need be, against the promptings of conscience and compassion. To do otherwise endangers the structure and enterprises of the whole.

After reading and discussing "A Confrontation in the Synagogue," you may present the class with Captain Vere's comments as an *amicus curiae* on behalf of Amaziah and institutionally obedient ushers. This example from "Billy Budd" may also help clarify the point that the ethical dilemma presented in this unit can and does arise in all types of institutions, not merely those we call religious.

BILLY BUDD

Scene I, Act III

Wyatt. Aye, that's it, sir. How can we condemn this man and live at peace again within ourselves? We have our standards; ethics, if you like.

Vere. Challenge your scruples! They move as in a dusk. Come, do they import something like this: if we are bound to judge, regardless of palliating circumstances, the death of Claggart as the prisoner's deed, then does that deed appear a capital crime whereof the penalty is mortal? But can we adjudge to summary and shameful death a fellow creature innocent before God, and whom we feel to be so? Does that state the case rightly?

Seymour. That is my feeling, sir.

Vere. You all feel, I am sure, that the boy in effect is innocent; that what he did was from an unhappy stricture of speech that made him speak with blows. And I believe that, too; believe as you do, that he struck his man down, tempted beyond endurance. Acquit him, then, you say, as innocent?

Ratcliffe. Exactly! Oh I know the Articles prescribe death for what Budd has done, but that …

Wyatt. Oh, stow the Articles! They don't account for such a case as this. You yourself say Budd is innocent.

Vere. In intent, Wyatt, in intent.

Wyatt. Does that count for nothing? His whole attitude, his motive, count for nothing? If his intent …

Vere. The intent or non-intent of Budd is nothing to the purpose. In a court more merciful than martial it would extenuate, and shall, at the last Assizes, set him free. But here we have these alternatives only: condemn or let go.

Seymour. But it seems to me we've got to consider the problem as a moral one, sir, despite the fact that we're not moralists. When Claggart told you his lie, the case immediately went beyond the scope of military justice.

Vere. I, too, feel that. But do these gold stripes across our arms attest that our allegiance is to Nature?

Ratcliffe. To our country, sir.

Vere. Aye, Ratcliffe; to the King. And though the sea, which is inviolate Nature primeval, though it be the element whereon we move and have our being as sailors, is our official duty hence to Nature? No. So little is that true that we resign our freedom when we put this on. And when war is declared, are we , the fighters commissioned to destroy, consulted first?

Wyatt. Does that deny us the right to act like men? We're not trying a murderer, a dockside cut-throat!

Vere. The gold we wear shows that we serve the King, the Law. What does it matter that our acts are fatal to our manhood, if we serve as we are forced to serve? What bitter salt leagues move between our code and God's own judgments! We are conscripts, every one, upright in this uniform of flesh. There is no truce to war born in the womb. We fight at command.

Wyatt. All I know is that I can't sit by and see Budd hanged!

Vere. I say we fight by order, by command of our superiors.

And if our judgments approve the war, it is only coincidence. And so it is with all our acts. So now, would it be so much we ourselves who speak as judges here, as it would be martial law operating through us? For that law, and for its rigor, we are not responsible. Our duty lies in this: that we are servants only.

Ratcliffe. The Admiralty doesn't want service like that. What good would it do? Who'd profit by Budd's death?

Wyatt. You want to make us murderers!

Seymour. Wyatt! Control yourself!

Vere. What is this vessel that you serve in, Wyatt, an ark of peace? Go count her guns; then tell your conscience to lie quiet, if you can.

Ratclilffe. But that is war. This would be downright killing!

Seymour. It's all war, Ratcliffe; war to the death, for all of us.

Vere. You see that, Seymour? That this war began before our time?

Seymour. And will end long after it.

Vere. Here we have the Mutiny Act for justice. No child can own a closer tie to parent than can that Act to what it stems from: War. This is a wartime cruise and in this ship are Englishmen who fight against their wills, perhaps against their conscience, 'pressed by war into the service of the King. Though we as fellow creatures understand their lot, what does it matter to the officer, or to the enemy? The French will cut down conscripts in the same swath with volunteers, and we will do as much for them. War has no business with anything but surfaces. War's child, the Mutiny Act, is featured like the father.

Ratcliffe. Couldn't we mitigate the penalty if we convict him?

Vere. No, Ratcliffe. The penalty is prescribed.

Ratcliffe. I would like to think it over, Captain. I'm not sure.

Vere. I repeat, then, that while we ponder and you hesitate over anxieties I confess to sharing, the enemy comes nearer. We must act, and quickly. The French close in on us; the crew will find out shortly what has happened. Our consciences are private matters, Ratcliffe. But we are public men, controlling life and death within this world at sea. Tell me whether or not in our positions we dare let our consciences take precedence of the code that makes us officers and calls this case to trial.

Ratcliffe. [after a pause; quietly] No, sir.

Wyatt. Can you stand Budd's murder on your conscience?

Seymour. Wyatt! Hold your tongue!

Wyatt. [jumping up] I say let him go!

Seymour. Sit down, sir!

Vere. Let him speak.

Wyatt. I won't bear a hand to hang a man I know is innocent! My blood's not cold enough. I can't give the kind of judgment you want to force on us! I ask to be excused from sitting upon this court.

Seymour. Do you know what you're saying? Sit down and hold your tongue, man!

Vere. The kind of judgment I ask of you is only this, Wyatt: that you recognize your function in this ship. I believe you know it quite as well as we, yet you rebel. Can't you see that you must first strip off the uniform you wear, and after that your flesh, before you can escape the case at issue here? Decide you must, Wyatt. Oh you may be excused and wash your hands of it, but someone must decide. We are the law, law orders us to act, and shows us how. Do you imagine Seymour, or Ratcliffe here, or I, would not save this boy if we could see a way consistent with our duties? Acquit Budd if you can. God knows I wish I could. If in your mind as well as in your heart, you can say freely that his life is not forfeit to the law we serve, reason with us! Show us how to save him without putting aside our function. Or if you can't do that, teach us to put by our responsibility and not betray ourselves. Can you do this? Speak, man, speak! Show us how! Save him, Wyatt, and you save us all. [WYATT slowly sits down.] You recognize the logic of the choice I force upon you. But do not think me pitiless in thus demanding sentence on a luckless boy. I feel as you do for him. But even more, I think there is a grace of soul within him that shall forgive the law we bind him with, and pity us, stretched on the cross of choice. [Turns away.]

Seymour. Well, gentlemen. Will you decide. [Officers write their verdicts on paper before them, and hand them to SEYMOUR, who rises, draws his dirk and places it on the table, pointing forward.] He is condemned, sir. Shall we appoint the dawn?

"Billy Budd" by Louis O. Coxe and Robert Chapman ©1947, 1949 and 1951 by Louis O. Coxe and Robert Chapman. Reprinted by permission of Farrar, Straus & Giroux, Inc.

Additional Sources

From the Bible

1. On priestly authority:

When the issue in any lawsuit is beyond your competence, whether it be a case of blood against blood, plea against plea, or blow against blow, that is disputed in your courts, then go up without delay to the place which the Lord your God will choose. There you must go to the Levitical priests or to the judge then in office; seek their guidance, and they will pronounce the sentence. You shall act on the pronouncement which they make from the place which the Lord shall choose. See that you carry out all their instructions. Act on the instruction which they give you, or on the precedent that they cite; do not swerve from what they tell you, either to right or to left. Anyone who presumes to reject the decision either of the priest who ministers there to the Lord your God, or of the judge, shall die; thus you will rid Israel of wickedness. Then all the people will hear of it and be afraid, and will never again show such presumption.

Deuteronomy 17:8

כי יפלא ממך דבר למשפט בין דם לדם בין דין לדין ובין נגע לנגע דברי ריבת בשעריך וקמת ועלית אל המקום אשר יבחר ה׳ אלוהיך בו ובאת אל הכהנים הלויים ואל השופט אשר יהיה בימים ההם ודרשת והגידו לך את דבר המשפט ועשית על פי הדבר אשר יגידו לך מן המקום ההוא אשר יבחר ה׳ ושמרת לעשות ככל אשר יורוך על פי התורה אשר יורוך ועל המשפט אשר יאמרו לך תעשה, לא תסור מן הדבר אשר יגידו לך ימין ושמאל והאיש אשר יעשה בזדון לבלתי שמוע אל הכהן העומד לשרת שם את ה׳ אלוהיך או אל השופט ומת האיש ההוא ובערת הרע מישראל (דברים יז).

2. On prophetic authority:

I will raise up for them a prophet like you, one of their own brethren, and I will put my words into his mouth. He shall convey all my commands to them, and if anyone does not listen to the words which he will speak in my name I will require satisfaction from him.

Deuteronomy 18:18

נביא אקים להם מקרב אחיהם כמוך ונתת דברי בפיו ודבר אלוהים את כל אשר אצוונו והיה האיש אשר לא ישמע אל דברי אשר ידבר בשמי אנכי אדרש מעמו (דברים יח).

3. Now two men named Eldad and Medad, who had been enrolled with the seventy, were left behind in the camp. But, though they had not gone out to the Tent, the spirit alighted on them none the less, and they fell into an ecstasy there in the camp. A young man ran and told Moses that Eldad and Medad were in an ecstasy in the camp, whereupon Joshua son of Nun, who had served with Moses since he was a boy, broke in, "My lord Moses, stop them!" but Moses said to him, "Are you jealous on my account? I wish that all the Lord's people were prophets and that the Lord would confer his spirit on them all." And Moses rejoined the camp with the elders of Israel.

Numbers 11:27

וירץ הנער ויגד למשה ויאמר אלדד ומידד מתנבאים במחנה ויען יהושע בן נון משרת משה מבחריו ויאמר אדני משה כלאם ויאמר לו משה המקנא אתה לי? ומי יתן כל עם הי נביאים כי יתן הי רוחו עליהם (במדבר יא).

From Rabbinic Literature

1. Rav, R. Chanina, R. Yochanan and R. Chaviva taught ... whoever can protest [the misdeeds of] one's household but does not, is held accountable for [the misdeeds of] the household; likewise with [the misdeeds of] those in one's town; likewise with [the misdeeds of] the whole world ..., R. Zera said to R. Simon, "Go, sir, and rebuke the members of the Exilarch's household." "They will not accept it from me," was his reply. "Though they may not accept it, rebuke them anyway, sir," he answered.

Shabbat 54-55

רב ורבי חנינא ורבי יוחנן ורב חביבא מתנו... כל מי שאפשר למחות לאנשי ביתו ולא מיחה נתפס על אנשי ביתו. באנשי עירו נתפס על אנשי עירו. בכל העולם כולו נתפס על כל העולם כולו... א״ל רי זירא לרי סימון לוכחינהו מר להני דבי ריש גלותא. א״ל לא מקבלי מינאי. א״ל אע״ג דלא מקבלי לוכחינהו מר (שבת נד).

2. *Tosaphot* on "though they may not accept it": In this case it is uncertain as to whether or not it [the rebuke] will be accepted ... but in a case where it is certain that it will not be accepted, it is better that they sin through ignorance than presumption.

תוספות: ״אע״ג דלא מקבלי לוכחינהו מר״:
היינו איכא דספק אי מקבלי כדאמר בסמוך
לפניהם מי גלוי אבל היכא דודאי לא מקבלי
הנח להם מוטב שיהו שוגגין ואל יהיו מזידין
כדאמרין ב״המביא כדי יין״.

3. "Leave the people of Israel alone: It is better that they sin through ignorance than presumption." This refers to Rabbinical prohibition, but does not apply in the case of a prohibition from the Torah.

Betzah 30

״המביא כדי יין״ (ביצה ל)
הנח להם לישראל. מוטב שיהיו שוגגין ואל יהיו
מזידין והני מילי בדרבנן אבל בדאורייתא לא.

4. Rab Judah said in Rab's name: Why was Avner punished? Because he could have protested to Saul (about the slaughter of the priests of Nob) but did not. R. Isaac, however, said: "He did protest but was not heeded." Both derive their views from the same verse: "And the King lamented for Avner and said: "Should Avner die as a churl dies, your hands were not bound nor your feet put into fetters." The one who says he did not protest interprets it in this way: "Your hands were not bound nor your feet put into fetters; why then didn't you protest?" ... The other who maintains that Avner *did* protest but was not heeded, interprets the verse as an expression of David's astonishment: "should he have died as a churl dies." Seeing as you did indeed protest to Saul, "Why, then, did you fall as a man falls before the children of sinners?" (*Sanhedrin 20a*)

As for Avner ben Ner — why was he killed? ... some say because he could have protested (the slaughter of the priests of) Nob but did not.

Numbers Rabbah XIX

מפני מה נענש אבנר? מפני שהיה לו למחות בשאול ולא
מיחה. רבי יצחק אמר: מיחה ולא נענה. ושניהן מקרא
אחד דרשו. ״ויקנן המלך אל אבנר ויאמר: הכמות נבל
ימות אבנר? ידך לא אסרות ורגליך לא לנחשתיים הגשו,
כנפול לפני בני עוולה נפלת״ (שמואל ב׳, ג:לג).
מאן דאמר לא מיחה - הכי כאמר: ידך לא אסרות ורגליך

לא לנחשתיים הוגשו, מאי טעמא לא מחית? "כנפול לפני בני עוולה נפלת". ומאן דאמר מיחה ולא נענה, איתמהו"י מתמה: הכמות נבל ימות? ידיך לא אסורות ורגליך לא לנחשתיים. מכדי מחויי מחית (סנה' כ).

ואבנר בן נר -- למה נהרג? ... י"א על שהיה בידו למחות על נוב ולא מיחה (במדבר ר', פ' חקת).

From *Sefer Hasidim* 107, 108

If someone prevents the *Sefer Torah* from being returned to the Ark by registering a complaint in the synagogue before the Ark, thereby attempting to force the congregation to do his will, the communal leaders should say, "You are acting illegally." That person's soul is destined to have the Torah cry out against it, "May so and so not rest in peace."

And if someone interrupts the *Amidah* the communal leaders should say, "You are acting illegally." And any one who does not heed them will not have the privilege of joining them in prayer in the world to come.

This advantage given plaintiffs sometimes allowed people with axes to grind to unduly disturb the congregation, to seek restitution in an illegal manner, and unnecessarily disrupt the daily service. Our Teachers therefore objected to anyone making a complaint in this manner.

(*Mekor Hesed, loc. cit.*).

ספר חסידים ק"ז, ק"ח:

כל המונע ס"ת מלהכניס לתוך ארון הקודש כגון הגובל בבית הכנסת לפני ההיכל וכן הרוצה להכריח ולדחוק את הקהל שיעשו חפצו וטובים אומרים שלא כדין אתה עושה עתידה תורה שתצעק ותכריז על נשמתו איש פלוני אל יבא למקום פלוני בשלום. ואם תעכב את התפילה והטובים אומרים שלא כדין אתה עושה ואינו שומע אליהם לעתיד לבא מתפללים ומשתחווים ולא יזכה להיות עמם.

והנה יפוי כח זה של התובע נתן לפעמים מקום לבעל מחלוקת לפסוע על ראשי עם קודש ולתבוע משפט שלא כדין ולבטל התמיד בלי הכרח. לכן ערער רבינו על הקובץ הזה (מקור חסד, שם).

A Modern Response

Halting Religious Services as a Protest

Question:

In a large Eastern congregation, it was decided a number of months ago, as an expression of good will, to honor President Hesburgh of Notre Dame University at the synagogue. Some time after the invitation was issued, Father Hesburgh announced a strict policy which he would follow against sit-ins at his university. He has received much publicity because of this statement. Since he has now become identified with a possibly strict policy against university sit-ins, a group in this eastern city has declared its intention to disrupt the religious services in the synagogue at which Father Hesburgh would be honored. Somebody encouraged this group by saying that there was actually a Jewish law which permits the services to be interrupted as a protest. What is this law, and does it justify the disruption of these services by such a group? (From Vigdor Kavaler, Pittsburgh, Pennsylvania.)

Answer:

The Palestinian Talmud (*J. Kedushin* I:7) gives the following narrative: Rabbi Jose and Rabbi Jonathan were studying together. A man came up to them, bent down, and kissed Rabbi Jonathan's feet. Jose then asked, "Why did this man kiss you so reverently? What favor did you do him?" Jonathan answered, "This man came to me and complained that his son refused to provide food for him. Thereupon I told the man to close the synagogue and not permit the services to proceed. The son was thus put to shame and thereafter provided food for his father."

It was, evidently, upon the basis of this narrative in the Talmud that the famous tenth-century Rhineland rabbinic leader, Rabbenu Gershom, the Light of the Exile, included among his various decrees the following one: If a man, though summoned to give testimony, refuses to obey the summons of the Jewish court, the aggrieved party (who needed the testimony for his defense) has the right at a certain point in the services to stop the services and thus, out of shame and community pressure, the recalcitrant witness would give in and consent to present his testimony.

This decree is recorded in the various early legal writings which transmit the decrees of Rabbenu Gershom, and various limitations were put upon this right of the aggrieved to stop the services. Some of the formulations of the decree speak also of community decrees, (Vitry, p. 799) which can be protested against, but this part of the elaboration of the decrees of Rabbenu Gershom was not developed nor cited in the later literature. The law as it is now found in the codes deals exclusively and only with the right of an aggrieved individual to protect his rights. It is mentioned in the Shulchan Aruch in quite an offhand way. In *Orach Chayim* 54, the question is dealt with as to whether one may converse between the second section of the morning prayer and the third or main section; i.e., between the prayer *Yishtabach* and the *Yotser (Barchu)*. Joseph Caro says it is a sin to interrupt with conversation at this point, but he adds: "However, some say that for the needs of the congregation or to supply charity, it is permitted to converse at this point." To this Isserles adds: "From this [permission] the custom has spread in many places to give prayers for the sick [at this spot in the service] and to complain in the synagogue that justice be done to him."

The whole custom seems always to be referred to in the words, "Some say," etc. So in Shulchan Aruch, *Choshen Mishpat* 5:2, Isserles says: "Some say that we may not complain in the synagogue during the month of Nisan nor during the 'Days of Awe.'"

Of course, this mode of spiritual pressure could only be effective in the days when it was a thing of horror to a community if it could not conduct or participate in any single one of a weekday's service (the first interruption had to be on a weekday service). And Moses Sofer of Pressburg (in his responsum, *Orach Chaim* #81) takes that as an evidence of the piety of the former days as compared to the lack of piety today, that merely stopping a weekday service could have created so great a public pressure against a stubborn witness that he would be forced to give his testimony.

It was soon evident that this power to stop the service could lend itself to great abuse. In fact, as early as the eleventh century, the *Sefer Chasidim*, also written in the Rhineland (edition Margolis, 107, 108) says that if the community heads tell the protester that his complaint is unjust, and if the protester persists, he forfeits the very future of his soul. And in the sixteenth century, one of the greatest rabbis of that period in Poland, Solomon Luria ("Maharshal," Responsa #20) had a case of a quarrel over the sale of kosher meat; after the case was adequately settled by the court, the complainant unjustly tried to stop the services and prevent the cantor from continuing. Luria protests against this abuse of an old privilege and says that he is resolved "to break the power of those who would abolish the service in the house of the Lord and say, 'Let this house be closed.'" See also the fine note by Reuben Margolis to *Sefer Chasidim*, #107.

In other words, this ancient privilege, which Rabbenu Gershom in the tenth century based upon the action of Rabbi Jonathan as reported in the Palestinian Talmud, was meant for the defense for a single aggrieved individual, and not as an opportunity for disruption by those whom Margolis calls *baale machloket*, "men of disputatiousness," nor to give them a forum by interrupting the service. It was not intended for them at all, but for an individual victim of injustice, and even this right was severely limited in the *Sefer Chasidim* and by Solomon Luria.

It is evident, therefore, that no organized group has the moral right, certainly not according to Jewish legal tradition, to interrupt the service as a mode of expressing their objection to the honoring of Father Hesburgh. And all decent, legal means should be taken to prevent such an unjustified disruption of the worship.

Modern Reform Responsa
by Solomon Freehof
(Cincinnati: Hebrew Union
College Press, 1971), 84-86.

Further Sources

1. A fine discussion of the legal and ethical ramifications of the confrontation between Amos and Amaziah can be found in "Amos vs. Amaziah" by Shalom Spiegel (J.T.S. Essays in Judaism Series, #3.)
2. An excellent general examination of moral responsibility, duty, law, authority and conscience is provided in "The Obligation to Disobey" by Mulford Q. Sibley New York: Conference on Religion and International Affairs, New York, 1970.
3. It was in fact an accepted practice in the medieval synagogue to interrupt services for redress of grievances. See *Jewish Life in the Middle Ages* by Israel Abrahams (New York: Meridian Books and Jewish Publication Society, 1958).
4. Another interesting analysis of the relationship between the priest and prophet is the essay "Priest and Prophet" in *Selected Essays* by Ahad Ha'am (Philadelphia: Jewish Publication Society, 1912), 125ff.
5. The song "Waist Deep in the Big Muddy" by Pete Seeger deals with the respose of soldiers to the orders of an officer. It can be found on the record "Waist Deep in the Big Muddy and Other Love Songs"(Columbia CS9505).

10th Grade – Adults

UNIT XIII

— The Birmingham Dilemma

לפנים משורת הדין

About This Unit

This concluding unit was designed with high school students in mind, but will certainly prove challenging to adults as well. The unit's dilemma raises the possibility that all the understandings of justice which characterize the first five stages of moral judgment may, in turn, be found lacking in comparison with a sixth, *most* adequate stage of reasoning. The basic characteristic of this sixth stage is a rationally arrived at commitment to a set of universal ethical principles — principles of human equality and respect for each individual as an *end, not a means* to any other goal.

Introduction for the Teacher

We usually consider the ability to abide by the law a salient feature of a morally mature individual. Societies are founded upon the supposition that there is a positive correlation between the quality of our life in society (also our self-image) and our ability to place personal goals within the parameters of community standards and expectations. In recognition of the positive role they are assumed to play in regulating social intercourse, these standards are endowed by the community, or by those who dominate the community, with an air of fundamental legitimacy. Depending upon its political structure, a group may allow such blanket legitimacy to accrue to acts of a monarch, court, legislature, voting majority, etc. Yet, each of us has, on occasion, come across a particular rule that we sense is not just, despite its being the law.

What faculty do we possess that senses this distinction between *law* and *justice*? Reinhold Niebuhr describes it this way:

> The social character of most moral judgments and the pressure of society upon an individual are both facts to be reckoned with; but neither explains the peculiar phenomenon of the moral life, usually called conscience ... men do possess, among other moral resources, a sense of obligation toward the good, as their mind conceives it ... It can be equated neither with the total dynamic character of life, nor with the individual's fear of the disapproval or discipline of his group ... Like conceptual knowledge it may be strengthened and enlarged by discipline, and may deteriorate by lack of use.[1]

Conscience is most apparent when there is something to lose, when some penalty militates against the conscience inspired act. Adversity tends to render acts transparent, allowing the intent behind the act to shine through more clearly. Therefore, to examine the ethical quality of an act of conscience, we must look at a situation in which it is countered by significant opposition. In the dilemma that follows, the protagonists' alleged act of conscience are tested against the penalties of law and custom. Those participants in the dilemmas who stand with the law, call for order within the law as it stands: "Who has put you above the law?" they protest. Their adversaries break the law in calling for a higher justice. Our task is to explore the role principles of conscience may play in such a confrontation. How does one formulate such principles? What may be the consequences of "following one's own lights" against the advice and sanctions of the community?

The Dilemma

Birmingham, Alabama was a thoroughly segregated city in April, 1963. Racial discrimination pervaded public life. Use of public accommodations, such as restrooms or lunch counters, was on a strictly segregated basis. Discriminatory hiring policies effectively kept Blacks out of certain types of jobs.

On April 3, 1963, a group of Birmingham's Black citizens, in cooperation with Dr. Martin Luther King, launched a campaign to achieve the following goals:

1. Removal of racial restrictions governing the use of downtown snack bars, restrooms and stores.
2. Ending of racially discriminatory hiring practices in certain job areas.
3. Formation of a biracial committee to plan for further desegregation in Birmingham.

The principal tactics of the campaign were sit-ins, marches and a boycott of merchants who discriminated.

On Wednesday, April 10 (second day of Pesach), the Alabama Supreme Court issued an injunction forbidding continued demonstrations while it investigated the Birmingham situation.

In response to this series of events, a statement was issued by eight prominent Birmingham clergymen calling for a halt to Dr. King's campaign.

On Friday, April 12, Martin Luther King, in violation of the Court's injunction, led a march to downtown Birmingham, and was arrested. While in jail, King composed a reply to the statement of the eight clergymen.

GO SLOW, DR. KING!

The following is a verbatim copy of the public statement directed to Martin Luther King, Jr. by eight Alabama clergymen, which elicited his reply which follows.

We the undersigned clergymen are among those who, in January, issued "An Appeal for Law and Order and Common Sense," in dealing with racial problems in Alabama. We expressed understanding that honest convictions in racial matters could properly be pursued in the courts, but urged that decisions of those courts should in the meantime be peacefully obeyed.

Since that time there had been some evidence of increased forbearance and a willingness to face facts. Responsible citizens have undertaken to work on various problems which cause racial friction and unrest. In Birmingham, recent public events have given indication that we all have opportunity for a new constructive and realistic approach to racial problems.

However, we are now confronted by a series of demonstrations by some of our Negro citizens, directed and led in part by outsiders. We recognize the natural impatience of people who feel that their hopes are slow in being realized. But we are convinced that these demonstrations are unwise and untimely.

We agree rather with certain local Negro leadership which has called for honest and open negotiation of racial issues in our area. And we believe this kind of facing of issues can best be accomplished by citizens of our own metropolitan area, white and Negro, meeting with their knowledge and experience of the local situation. All of us need to face that responsibility and find proper channels for its accomplishment.

Just as we formerly pointed out that "hatred and violence have no sanction in our religious and political traditions," we also point out that such actions as incite to hatred and violence, however technically peaceful those actions may be, have not contributed to the resolution of our local problems. We do not believe that these days of new hope are days when extreme measures are justified in Birmingham.

We commend the community as a whole, and the local news media and law enforcement officials in particular, on the calm manner in which these demonstrations have been handled. We urge the public to continue to show restraint should the demonstrations continue, and the law enforcement officials to remain calm and continue to protect our city from violence.

We further strongly urge our own Negro community to withdraw support from these demonstrations, and to unite locally in working peacefully for a better Birmingham. When rights are consistently denied, a cause should be pressed in the courts and in negotiations among local leaders, and not in the streets. We appeal to both our white and Negro citizenry to observe the principles of law and order and common sense.

(The eight clergymen who issued this statement were: Bishop C.C.J. Carpenter, Bishop Joseph A. Durick, Rabbi Milton L. Grafman, Bishop Nolan B. Harmon, Rev. George H. Murray, Rev. Edward Ramage, Rev. Earl Stallings.)

LETTER FROM BIRMINGHAM JAIL

April 16, 1963
Birmingham, Alabama

My Dear Fellow Clergymen:

While confined here in the Birmingham city jail, I came across your recent statement calling my present activities "unwise and untimely." Seldom do I pause to answer criticism of my work and ideas. If I sought to answer all the criticisms that cross my desk, my secretaries would have little time for anything other than such correspondence in the course of the day, and I would have no time for constructive work. But since I feel that you are men of genuine good will and that your criticisms are sincerely set forth, I want to try to answer your statement in what I hope will be patient and reasonable terms.

... I, along with several members of my staff, am here because I was invited here. I am here because I have organizational ties here ... Moreover, I am cognizant of the interrelatedness of all communities and states. I cannot sit idly by in Atlanta and not be concerned about what happens in Birmingham. Injustice anywhere is a threat to justice everywhere. We are caught in an inescapable network of mutuality, tied in a single garment of destiny. Whatever affects one directly, affects all indirectly. Never again can we afford to live with the narrow provincial "outside agitator" idea. Anyone who lives inside the United States can never be considered an outsider anywhere within its bounds.

You deplore the demonstrations taking place in Birmingham. But your statement, I am sorry to say, fails to express a similar concern for the conditions that brought about the demonstrations. I am sure that none of you would want to rest content with the superficial kind of social analysis that deals merely with effects and does not grapple with underlying causes. It is unfortunate that demonstrations are taking place in Birmingham, but it is even more unfortunate that the city's white power structure left the Negro community with no alternative.

... My friends, I must say to you that we have not made a single gain in civil rights without determined legal and nonviolent pressure. Lamentably, it is an historical fact that privileged groups seldom give up their privileges voluntarily. Individuals may see the moral light and voluntarily give up their unjust posture; but, as Reinhold Niebuhr has reminded us, groups tend to be more immoral than individuals.

You express a great deal of anxiety over our willingness to break laws. This is certainly a legitimate concern. Since we so diligently urge people to obey the Supreme Court's decision of 1954 outlawing segregation in the public schools, at first glance it may seem rather paradoxical for us consciously to break laws. One may well ask: "How can you advocate breaking some laws and obeying others?" The answer lies in the fact that there are two types of laws: just and unjust. I would be the first to advocate obeying just laws. One has not only a legal but a moral responsibility to obey just laws. Conversely, one has a moral responsibility to disobey unjust laws. I would agree with St. Augustine that "an unjust law is no law at all."

Now, what is the difference between the two? How does one determine whether a law is just or unjust? A just law is a man-made code that squares with the moral law or the law of God. An unjust law is a code that is out of harmony with the moral law. To put it in the terms of St. Thomas Aquinas: An unjust law is a human law that is not rooted in eternal law and natural law. Any law that uplifts human personality is just. Any law that degrades human personality is unjust. All segregation statutes are unjust because segregation distorts the soul and damages the personality. It gives the segregator a false sense of superiority and the segregated a false sense of inferiority. Segregation, to use the terminology of the Jewish philosopher Martin Buber, substitutes an "I-It" relationship for an "I-Thou" relationship and ends up relegating persons to the status of things. Hence segregation is not only politically, economically, and sociologically unsound, it is morally wrong and sinful: Paul Tillich has said that sin is separation. Is not segregation an existential expression of man's tragic separation, his awful estrangement, his terrible sinfulness? Thus it is that I can urge men to obey the 1954 decision of the supreme Court, for it is morally right; and I can urge them to disobey segregation ordinances, for they are morally wrong.

Let us consider a more concrete example of just and unjust laws. An unjust law is a code that a numerical or power majority group compels a minority group to obey but does not make binding on itself. This is *difference* made legal. By the same token, a just law is a code that a majority compels a minority to follow and that it is willing to follow itself. This is sameness made legal.

... Sometimes a law is just on its face and unjust in its application. For instance, I have been arrested on a charge of parading without a permit. Now, there is nothing wrong in having an ordinance which required a permit for a parade. But such an ordinance becomes unjust when it is used to maintain segregation and to deny citizens the First Amendment privilege of peaceful assembly and protest.

I hope you are able to see the distinction I am trying to point out. In no sense do I advocate evading or defying the law, as would the rabid segregationist. That would lead to anarchy. One who breaks an unjust law must do so openly, lovingly, and with a willingness to accept the penalty. I submit that an individual who breaks a law that conscience tells him is unjust, and who willingly accepts the penalty of imprisonment in order to arouse the conscience of the community over its injustice, is in reality expressing the highest respect for the law.

Of course, there is nothing new about this kind of civil disobedience. It was evidenced sublimely in the refusal of Shadrach,

Meshach, and Abednego to obey the laws of Nebuchadnessar, on the ground that a higher moral law was at stake. It was practiced superbly by the early Christians, who were willing to face hungry lions and the excruciating pain of chopping blocks rather than submit to certain unjust laws of the Roman Empire. To a degree, academic freedom is a reality today because Socrates practiced civil disobedience. In our own nation, the Boston Tea Party represented a massive act of civil disobedience.

We should never forget that everything Adolf Hitler did in Germany was "legal" and everything the Hungarian freedom fighters did in Hungary was "illegal." It was "illegal" to aid and comfort a Jew in Hitler's Germany. Even so, I am sure that, had I lived in Hitler's Germany at the time, I would have aided and comforted my Jewish brothers. If today I lived in a Communist country where certain principles dear to the Christian faith are suppressed, I would openly advocate disobeying that country's anti-religious laws ...

It is true that the police have exercised a degree of discipline in handling the demonstrators. In this sense they have conducted themselves rather "nonviolently" in public. But for what purpose? To preserve the evil system of segregation. Over the past few years I have consistently preached that nonviolence demands that the means we must use must be as pure as the ends we seek. I have tried to make clear that it is wrong, or perhaps even more so, to use moral means to preserve immoral ends. Perhaps Mr. Connor and his policemen have been rather nonviolent in public, as was Chief Pritchett in Albany, Georgia, but they have used the moral means of nonviolence to maintain the immoral end of racial injustice. As T.S. Eliot has said, "The last temptation is the greatest treason: to do the right deed for the wrong reason."

I wish you had commended the Negro sit-inners and demonstrators of Birmingham for their sublime courage, their willingness to suffer, and their amazing discipline in the midst of great provocation. One day the South will recognize its real heroes .... One day the South will know that when these disinherited children of God sat down at lunch counters, they were in reality standing up for what is best in the American dream and for the most sacred values in our Judaeo-Christian heritage. Yours for the cause of Peace and Brotherhood,

Martin Luther King

Dilemma Question

Suppose you are a Rabbi in Birmingham, Alabama in 1963. You have been approached by supporters of Dr. King to join in a march to downtown Birmingham tomorrow. You have also been asked by the eight clergymen who issued the "unwise and untimely" statement to add your name to the appeal and to disassociate yourself from Dr. King's campaign. What would you do?

Suggested Procedure

1. Briefly describe the topic of the unit to your class. For instance: How do you ultimately decide what is right and wrong? Is there a higher moral standard than democratically determined law? If so, what is to be done if you see this higher standard contradicting the demands of certain laws or customs of your society?
2. Read together "Information for the Birmingham Dilemma" below. If you want more specifics on the Birmingham situation, you may wish to consult sources noted in the Additional Sources below.
3. This unit's dilemma is formed by two documents — (1) a statement by eight Birmingham, Alabama clergymen critical of Dr. Martin Luther King's activities in their city in April 1963 and (2) Dr. King's response. Read the statement of the clergymen first, then Dr. King's Apologia. Discuss the dilemma question that follows the two documents.
4. Here are some possible follow-up questions for the discussion.
   (For those who said they would join the demonstration)
   a. One of your congregants asks: "What gives you the right to tell me that I am obligated to follow the laws of the Torah (or rules of the synagogue or school) seeing that you have chosen to ignore the laws of the state?" How would you respond?
   b. Consider: If you were to join Dr. King's demonstration, you could very well be dismissed by your congregation and replaced by someone less concerned than you are about human rights. You will then have lost any chance of positively influencing your congregation. Should the sensitivities of your congregation play any part in your decision? (See Additional Sources #4)
   c. Would you refrain from joining the march if:
      1) the leaders of the demonstration were not committed to non-violence.
      2) the leaders of the demonstration were anti-Semitic?

   (For those who said they would sign the ad)
   a. Would you join the march if:
      1) the majority of your congregants asked you to join it?
      2) the laws in Birmingham were directly discriminatory toward Jews also?

3) the director of the Alabama Rabbinical Association directed you to join it?
4) you had agreed to participate fully with Dr. King's campaign before the injunction was issued?

5. Do the supplementary exercise.
6. Examine some of the supplementary materials.

Cue Sheet

Below, on the left, are some points your students might bring up in the course of discussing this unit's dilemma. On the right you'll find some suggested responses to these comments. These critical responses are designed to help focus discussion on possible weaknesses or contradictions in the reasoning which led to the initial comment. It is most often preferable that these sorts of responses come from other classmates, but if such challenges are not forthcoming, you yourself should provide them.

Student Statements	Possible Teacher Response
1. When the laws aren't obeyed, you end up with chaos. If each individual were allowed to choose which laws he or she would obey, society would disintegrate.	1. An unjust social order, maintained by brute force, is no order at all. In fact, it is a sort of moral chaos. The court can't have it both ways: either Black people are not a part of "We, the people" and are therefore not obligated to follow the law at all, or Black people have the same "inalienable," constitutionally guaranteed rights as any other American, including the right to assemble peaceably. If the latter is so, the court may not prohibit them from exercising those rights.
2. If I were in Dr. King's place, I'd want others to help demonstrate for my *rights*.	2. A Rabbi's first responsibility is to his or her congregation. A Rabbi must be very careful not to embarrass or endanger his or her congregants.

3. There are democratic/legal ways to change the law. A person can't take the law into his or her own hands.

3. But most Black people living in the South at that time were not allowed to vote. And even if they could have voted, they were still a minority. Does the majority rule, even at the expense of the minority's rights?

4. Doesn't Judaism teach that "the law of the government is the law?"

4. Numerous cases could be cited to show that *dina d'malchuta dina* does not mean that Jews should submit to tyranny, e.g., Moses in Egypt, Akiba's support of the revolt against Rome, etc.

5. If I were a Black, I might join the demonstration, but since I'm a Jew, I really don't think it's my fight.

5. It is our fight, too. Democratic institutions collapse if we are not mutually supportive of each other's basic human rights, and we all rely on and benefit from those institutions.

Supplementary Exercise

In the letter from a Birmingham Jail, Dr. King states: "An unjust law is a code that is out of harmony with the moral law . . . a human law that is not rooted in eternal law and natural law." Perhaps the most extraordinary evidence that the Torah also knows of a transcendent moral law is found in Genesis 18:16-33. Our attention should in particular be drawn to Abraham's statement: Shall not the judge of all the world do justly (Genesis 18:25)? Here Abraham judges God's impending action by an objective standard which both he and God apparently acknowledge as legitimate: the standard of *mishpat* (justice). *Mishpat* in this context appears to mean something akin to Dr. King's "moral law."

Have the class read Genesis 18:16-22. Ask: What does Abraham mean by *mishpat*? Point out: If *mishpat* means "following the law," to what law could Abraham be referring? Remember, the Torah had not yet been revealed ... or had it?! Relate the discussion to King's comments on "moral law ... eternal law and natural law."

Additional Sources

1. The following three statements touch upon the relationship between Jewish values and civil disobedience. The first is an open letter drafted by 16 Rabbis in the course of an act of civil disobedience in St. Augustine, Florida, issued June 19, 1964. The second is a statement from the Synagogue Council of America. The third is a selection from Judaism Eternal, a collection of essays by Rabbi Samson Raphael Hirsch.

Open Letter From Sixteen Rabbis: Why We Went

St. Augustine is the oldest city in the United States. It was here on St. Augustine's Day, August 28, 1565, that Pedro Menendez de Aviles first sighted land. In 1965 it will celebrate its 400th anniversary — indeed it has requested federal funds to enhance this historic observance. St. Augustine has other distinguishing characteristics. In American history books yet to be written, this small, neatly kept Florida community will long be remembered as a symbol of a harsh, rigidly segregated, Klan-dominated, backward-looking city which mocked the spirit of the doughty African-born, dark pigmented priest for whom it was named.

St. Augustine is a tourist town. By far the highest percentage of its income comes from the visitors who walk through its quaint streets staring at "excavations" from the 18th century only now being restored. Most visitors stop at the Slave Market, supposedly only a relic of bygone days. True, they no longer sell slaves in that market, but let no one be deceived into thinking that there no longer exists among this town's white residents the mental attitude and the psychology which first put slaves on those trading blocks. The spirit of racial arrogance persists and is reinforced by the sway of terror long exerted by hooded and unhooded mobsters.

We went to St. Augustine in response to the appeal of Martin Luther King addressed to the CCAR conference, in which he asked us to join with him in a creative witness to our joint convictions of equality and racial justice.

We came because we realized that injustice in St. Augustine, as anywhere else, diminishes the humanity of each of us. If St. Augustine is to be not only an ancient city but also a great-hearted city, it will not happen until the raw hate, the ignorant prejudices, the unrecognized fears which now grip so many of its citizens are exorcised from its soul. We came then, not as tourists, but as ones who, perhaps quixotically, thought we could add a bit to the healing process of America.

We were arrested on Thursday, June 18, 1964. Fifteen of us were arrested while praying in an integrated group in front of Monson's Restaurant. Two of us were arrested for sitting down at a table with three Negro youngsters in the Chimes Restaurant. We pleaded not guilty to the charges against us.

Shortly after our confinement in the St. John's County Jail, we shared with one another our real, inner motives. They are, as might be expected, mixed. We have tried to be honest with one another about the wrong, as well as the right, motives which have prompted us. These hours have been filled with a sense of surprise and discovery, of fear and affirmation, of self-doubt and belief in God.

We came to St. Augustine mainly because we could not stay away. We could not say no to Martin Luther King, whom we always respected and admired and whose loyal friends we hope we shall be in the days to come. We could not pass by the opportunity to achieve a moral goal by moral means — a rare modern privilege — which has been the glory of the non-violent struggle for civil rights.

We came because we could not stand silently by our brother's blood. We had done that too many times before. We have been vocal in our exhortation of others but the idleness of our hands too often revealed an inner silence; silence at a time when silence has become the unpardonable sin of our time. We came in the hope that the God of us all would accept our small involvement as partial atonement for the many things we wish we had done before and often.

We came as Jews who remember the millions of faceless who stood quietly, watching the smoke rise from Hitler's crematoria. We came because we know that, second only to silence, the greatest danger to man is loss of faith in man's capacity to act.

Here in St. Augustine we have seen the depths of anger, resentment, and fury: we have seen faces that expressed a deep implacable hatred. What disturbs us more deeply is the large number of decent citizens who have stood aside, unable to bring themselves to act, yet knowing in their hearts that this cause is right and that it must inevitably triumph.

We believe, though we could not count on it in advance, that our presence and actions here have been of practical effect. They have reminded the embattled Negroes here that they are not isolated and alone. The conscience of the wicked has been troubled, while that of the righteous has gained new strength. We are more certain than before that this cause is invincible, but we also have a sharpened awareness of the great effort and sacrifice which will be required. We pray that what we have done may lead us on to further actions and persuade others who still stand hesitantly to take the stand they know is just.

We came from different backgrounds and with different degrees of involvement. Some of us have had intimate experience with the struggle of minority groups to achieve full and equal rights in our widely scattered home communities. Others of us have had less direct contact with the underprivileged and the socially oppressed. And yet for all of us these brief, tension-packed hours of openness and communication turned an abstract social issue into something personal and immediate. We shall not forget the people with whom we drove, prayed, marched, slept, ate, demonstrated, and were arrested. How little we know of these people and their struggle. What we have learned has changed us and our attitudes. We are grateful for the rare experience of sharing with this courageous community in their life, their suffering, their effort. We pray that we may remain more sensitive and more alive as a result.

We shall not soon forget the stirring and heartfelt excitement with which the Negro community greeted us with full-throated hymns and hallelujahs, which pulsated and resounded through the church; nor the bond of affectionate solidarity which joined us hand in hand during our marches through town; nor the exaltation which lifted our voices and hearts in unison; nor the common purpose which transcended our fears as well as all the boundaries of race, geography, and circumstance. We hope we have strengthened the morale of St. Augustine Negroes as they strive to claim their dignity and humanity; we know they have strengthened ours.

Each of us has in this experience become a little more the person, a bit more the rabbi he always hoped to be (but has not yet been able to become).

We believe in man's ability to fulfill God's commands with God's help. We make no messianic estimate of man's power and certainly not of what we did here. But it has reaffirmed our faith in the significance of the deed. So we must confess in all humility that we did this as much in fulfillment of our faith and in response to inner need as in service to our Negro brothers. We came to stand with our brothers and in the process have learned more about ourselves and our God. In obeying Him, we become ourselves; in following His will we fulfill ourselves. He had guided, sustained, and strengthened us in a way we could not manage on our own.

We are deeply grateful to the good influences which have sustained us in our moments of trial and friendship. Often we thought of parents, wives, children, congregants, particularly our teenage youth, and of our teachers and our students. How many a Torah reading, Passover celebration, prayer book text and sermonic effort has come to mind in these hours. And how meaningful has been our worship, morning and evening, as we recited the ancient texts in this new, yet Jewishly familiar, setting. We are particularly grateful for what we have received from our comrades in this visit. We have been sustained by the understanding, thoughtfulness, consideration, and good humor we have received from each other. Never have the bonds of Judaism and the fellowship of the rabbinate been more clearly expressed to us all or more deeply felt by each of us.

These words were first written at 3:00 a.m. in the sweltering heat of a sleepless night, by the light of the one naked bulb hanging in the corridor outside our small cell. They were, ironically, scratched on the back of the pages of a mimeographed report of the bloody assaults of the Ku Klux Klan in St. Augustine. At daybreak we revised the contents of the letter and prayed together for a new dawn of justice and mercy for all the children of God.

We do not underestimate what yet remains to be done, in the north as well as the south. In the battle against racism, we have participated here in only a skirmish. But the total effect of all such demonstrations has created a revolution: and the conscience of the nation has been aroused as never before. The Civil Rights Bill will become law and much more progress will be attained because this national conscience has been touched in this and other places in the struggle.

We praise and bless God for His mighty acts on our behalf.

Baruch ata Adonai matir asurim. Blessed art Thou, O Lord, who freest the captives.

Reprinted from *Jewish Values and Social Crisis: A Casebook for Social Action* by Albert Vorspan (New York: Union of American Hebrew Congregations, 1968).

A Statement from the Synagogue Council of America

Respect for the law is deeply ingrained in the texture of Judaism. While fully aware of the transfiguring power of love in the affairs of men, Judaism has never accepted the thesis that love supersedes the law and that human society can dispense with the legal order in its search for justice. Cognizant of the potential for chaos and violence in the absence of governmental authority where each man does that which is right in his eyes, the Jewish tradition, from ancient times, called on its adherents to give thanks to God the Creator for the institution of government and for the rule of law that is thereby made possible. Consequently, Judaism cannot view lightly the actions of those who feel free to violate laws that do not meet with their approval. This is particularly so in a democratic order which clearly cannot be preserved unless dissenters, in deference to the social contract, respect the will of the majority as expressed in law even in those instances where the convictions of the minority dissent from those of the majority. It is clear that no system of law is possible where each man is obliged to obey only those laws that correspond to his views.

At the same time, Judaism considers each individual personally responsible before God for his actions. No man who violates the eternal will of the Creator can escape responsibility by pleading that he acted as an agent of another, whether that other be an individual or the state. It is therefore possible, under unusual circumstances, for an individual to find himself compelled by conscience to reject the demands of a human law which to the individual in question appears to conflict with the demand made on him by a higher law. Because the laws of most states in history have not made special provision for the conscientious objector, such individuals usually had to pay the price exacted of those who violated the laws of the state. It is one of the glories of American democracy that conscientious objection to war is recognized by the law as worthy of respect and that those who harbor such objections to all wars are permitted to fulfill their obligations by means that do not conflict with their consciences.

Statement by Rabbi Hirsch

The Talmud pledges the Jew to be loyal to the country of which he is a citizen, to love it as his fatherland and to promote its welfare, as Jeremiah laid down at the time of the Babylonian Captivity: "And seek the peace of the city whither I have caused you to be carried away captives, and pray unto the Lord for it, for in the peace thereof shall ye have peace" (Jeremiah 29:5-7). That has been the

Jewish guiding principle always and everywhere. "The law of the land is law"; in this concise statement the Talmud lays down the norm for our behavior. It means that the law enacted by the government of the state in which we live and whose subjects we are is binding upon us also from the religious point of view. Never leave the respect due to the state out of your sight. Pray for the welfare of the state, for were it not for fear of the state, society would be dissolved in a war of all against all.

JUDAISM ETERNAL, Vol. II
by Samson Raphael Hirsch (London: Soncino Press, Ltd., 1956).

2. Conscience in Traditional Jewish Literature

The Hebrew Bible in a variety of ways refers to what we have here called "conscience." Some, though not all, uses of *Yir'at Ha-shem* (fear of God) suggest a meaning akin to "conscience" (Genesis 20:11). Often, conscience is seen as one of the functions of the heart or kidneys, as when David was "struck by his heart" (II Samuel 24:10). Sometimes conscience must be inferred, as in the case of Abraham's concern over the fate of Sodom (Genesis 18:16-33). In Rabbinic literature the term *yetzer ha-tov* was employed to describe such innate moral impulses and promptings.

Modern Hebrew uses the word *matzpun* for "conscience," but this usage is neither biblical nor Rabbinic. Incidently, the use of the English term "conscience" in this sense is also relatively recent, dating back only a couple of centuries.

3. Sources for information on the 1963 Birmingham Civil Rights Campaign
   a. *Portrait of a Decade: The Second American Revolution* by Anthony Lewis (New York: Random House, 1964), Chapter 10.
   b. *Jewish Values and Social Crisis* by Albert Vorspan (New York: Union of American Hebrew Congregations, 1968), 111-131.
   c. The complete text of "Letter From a Birmingham Jail" can be found in *Why We Can't Wait* by Martin Luther King (New York: Harper and Row, 1963), Chapter 5.
   d. Several informative articles on conscience, natural law, civil disobedience, etc. appear in *Contemporary Jewish Ethics* by Menachem Marc Kellner (New York: Sanhedrin Press 1978).
   e. For Rabbinic material which is also relevant to this unit, see Additional Sources for Unit XI – Social Contract.

4. A book entitled *Scottsboro: A Tragedy of the American South* by Dan T. Carter (Baton Rouge: Louisiana University Press, 1979) describes what occurred when, in 1931, a Rabbi from Montgomery, Alabama, came to the defense of the so-called "Scottsboro Boys" — nine young Black men who were convicted, under the most questionable of circumstances, of raping two white women. His unpopular stand on a highly controversial issue parallels this unit's dilemma story in many of its specifics and may serve as an historical example of the possible consequences of taking such a stand.

AFTERWORD

Moral education is not simply another item on the already cluttered agenda of Jewish education — it is of its essence. Our values define us as a people: "Anyone who has compassion upon creatures is certainly a descendant of Abraham our father, and anyone who does not have compassion upon creatures is certainly not a descendant of Abraham our father" (*Betza* 32b).

Maimonides concludes his *Guide* with the assertion that though true human perfection is intellectual, the unmistakable fruit of that perfection is that through the intellect one is constantly drawn to doing acts of *chesed, mishpat* and *tzedekah* . "For in this alone may one take pride: in knowing Me and realizing that I, the Lord, do *chesed, mishpat* and *tzedekah* on earth, for in these I take delight, says the Lord" (Jeremiah 9:23). May we learn to make these ideals our desire as well.

ENDNOTES

INTRODUCTION

1. Lawrence Kohlberg, "Education, Moral Development, and Faith," *Journal of Moral Education* (January, 1975): 5.
2. Moshe M. Blatt and Lawrence Kohlberg, "The Effects of Classroom Moral Discussion Upon Children's Level of Moral Judgement," *Journal of Moral Education* (February, 1975): 129.
3. Kohlberg, "Education, Moral Development, and Faith," 9.
4. See note 3 above.
5. Saadia Gaon, Introduction to *Emunot V'Deot.*
6. *Chovot Halivavot,* Introduction.
7. *Jerusalem Talmud, Peah* 2:6.
8. Lawrence Kohlberg, *The Philosophy of Moral Development* (San Francisco: Harper and Row, 1981): 9.
9. Kohlberg, *The Philosophy of Moral Development,* 409.
10. *Mishnah Commentary: Perek Helek.*
11. Kohlberg, "Education, Moral Development, and Faith," 14.
12. *Kiddushin* 40b.
13. Kohlberg, *The Philosophy of Moral Development,* 352.
14. Ibid., 354.
15. See Brian Hayden and Daniel Pickar, "The Impact of Moral Discussions on Children's Level of Moral Reasoning," *Journal of Moral Education* 10 (February 1981): 131-134.

UNIT I

1. Dr. Joseph Hertz, *The Pentateuch and Haftorahs* (London: Soncino, 1960), 10.
2. See Maimonides' *Guide of the Perplexed,* III 54 (Chicago: University of Chicago Press Edition, Volume II), 635, paragraph 1.
3. Research suggests that "fair exchange" is the first nonpersonal moral standard most children grasp. This makes "fairness" the most developmentally appropriate standard with which to challenge a simple obedience-punishment orientation.

UNIT V

1. See Additional Sources for Unit V for Maimonides' complete definition.

UNIT VI

1. Gordon W. Allport, *The Nature of Prejudice* (New York: Anchor Books, 1958), 325. The term "scapegoat" is derived from the biblically prescribed ceremony in which the sins of the people of

Israel were symbolically purged by their ritual transference to an innocent and arbitrarily chosen goat (Leviticus 16). (See Additional Sources for this unit.)

UNIT VII

1. Genesis 2:25, 3:1.
2. *Targum Yonatan* on Genesis 2:25, 3:1.
3. Genesis 3:11-13.

UNIT X

1. *Statesman*, trans. J.B. Skemp (New Haven: Yale University Press, 1952), 249b.
2. Ibid., 295a.

UNIT XI

1. *Harijan*, 27 May 1939. (Indian newspaper)

UNIT XIII

1. Reinhold Niebuhr, *Moral Man and Immoral Society* (New York: Scribners, 1932) 36-38.

BIBLIOGRAPHY

Books

Fowler, James W. *Stages of Faith,* New York: Harper and Row, 1981.

Fowler is the leading theorist of faith development. Kohlberg has embraced Fowler's work.

Galbraith, Ronald E. and Jones, Thomas M. *Moral Reasoning: A Teaching Handbook for Adapting Kohlberg to the Classroom.* St. Paul: Greenhaven Press, 1976.

A good practical guide to the dilemma-discussion method, Includes practical methods for constructing dilemmas and a collection of dilemmas.

Hass, Glen, Editor. *Curriculum Planning: A New Approach,* Boston: Allyn and Bacon, Inc., 1974.

A fine collection of articles on curriculum planning, including several articles on the cognitive development approach.

Kohlberg, Lawrence. *Moral Stages and the Idea of Justice, Vol. 1, Essays on Moral Development.* San Francisco: Harper and Row, 1981.

This is the first in a projected three volume anthology of Kohlberg's writings. Includes a complete bibliography of Kohlberg's writings.

Articles

Adams, Dennis, "Building Moral Dilemma Activities." *Learning* (March 1977): 44-46.

Some good practical suggestions on presenting and discussing moral dilemmas. Also includes several sample dilemmas with accompanying "probe questions."

Blatt, Moshe M. and Kohlberg, Lawrence. "The Effects of Classroom Moral Discussion Upon Children's Level of Moral Judgement." *Journal of Moral Education* 4 (February 1975): 129-161.

This research report includes a brief description of a pilot moral development program in a Jewish Sunday School.

Chazan, Barry. "Jewish Education and Moral Development." In *Kohlberg and Moral Education: The Debate in Philosophy, Psychology,*

Religion and Education, Brenda Muncie, ed. Birmingham, Alabama: Religious Education Press, 1980, 298-325.

In this article, Chazan maintains that Kohlberg's cognitive developmental approach is largely irrelevant to Jewish moral education.

Galbraith, Ronald and Jones, Thomas M. "Teaching Strategies for Moral Dilemmas: An Application of Kohlberg's Theory of Moral Development to the Social Studies Classroom." *Social Education*, Vol. 39, No. 1 (January 1975): 16-22.

Gilligan, C. "In a Different Voice: Women's Conceptions of Self and Morality." *Harvard Educational Review* 47 (1977): 481-517.

In this article, Carol Gilligan, a former research associate of Kohlberg's, presents her finding on differences between male and female expressions of moral judgment.

Kohlberg, Lawrence. "Collected Papers on Moral Development and Moral Education." Center for Moral Education, 3rd floor, Larsen Hall, Harvard University, Cambridge, MA 02138.

Many of the essays in this early collection of articles (1973) have been published again in the first volume of Kohlberg's collected essays (see Books).

Kohlberg, Lawrence. "Education, Moral Development, and Faith." *Journal of Moral Education* 4 (January 1975): 5-16.

An edited version of an address to the National Catholic Education Association in which Kohlberg discusses the relationship between faith and moral development.

Rest, James. "Developmental Psychology as a Guide to Value Education: A Review of Kohlbergian Programs. *Review of Educational Research* 44 (No. 2. 1974): 241-258.

Rosenzweig, Linda W. "Toward Universal Justice: Some Implications of Lawrence Kohlberg's Research for Jewish Education." *Jewish Education*. Vol. 45. No. 3 (Summer-Fall 1977): 13-19.

An overview of Kohlberg's levels and stages of moral development with recommendations for awareness of his theories in relationship to Jewish learning, specifically in the areas of ethics and history.

Rossel, Seymour. "Lawrence Kohlberg and the Teaching of Jewish Ethics." *Jewish Education*, Vol. 45, No. 3 (Summer-Fall 1977): 20-23.

An excellent article which punctures holes in Kohlberg's theories as they pertain to Jewish education. Rossel charges Kohlberg with secularizing morality.

Saxton, Martha. "Are Women More Moral than Men? An Interview with Psychologist Carol Gilligan." *Ms. Magazine*, Vol 10, #6 (December 1981): 63-66.

This brief interview provides an overview of Gilligan's research on female moral judgment.

Schein, Jeff. "Lawrence Kohlberg's Theory of Moral Development: Some Implications for Jewish Schools." *Alternatives*, Winter 1978.

Briefly reviews Kohlberg's theory and suggests how it might be applicable to Jewish education.

Schnaidman, Mordecai. "Values in Orthodox Yeshivot and Day Schools." *Pedagogic Reporter* 32 (Fall 1980): 16-19.

Briefly analyzes some of the more prominent needs and resources in Jewish moral education.

Social Education. Vol. 40, No. 4 (April 1976): 213-215.

This issue contains a special section on the cognitive developmental approach to moral education, including an introduction by Kohlberg and an extensive bibliography.

Sosevsky, Moshe Chaim. "Kohlberg Moral Dilemmas and Jewish Moral Education." *Jewish Education*, Vol. 48, No. 4 (Winter 1980): 10-13.

The author suggests adapting Kohlberg's theories to Jewish education by presenting *midrashic* and *halachic* data along with the dilemmas.

Dissertations

Glosser, Joanne Katz. "Moral Development in Jewish Education: In Search of a Synthesis." Masters Degree Thesis, Hebrew Union College-Jewish Institute of Religion, Los Angeles, 1977.

Menitoff, Michael. "A Comparative Study of Moral Development in Jewish Religious School Settings." Ph.D. dissertation, U.C.L.A., 1977.

Rosenzweig, Linda W. "Moral Dilemmas in Jewish History." Ph.D. dissertation, Carnegie Mellon University, 1975.

Schein, Jeffrey, "Genesis and In Their Footsteps: An Evaluation of Two Programs in Moral Education Designed for Jewish Schools." Ph.D. dissertation, Temple University, 1981.

Shawver, D.J. "Character and Ethics: An Epistomological Inquiry of Lawrence Kohlberg's Cognitive Theory of Moral Development." Ph.D. dissertation, McGill University, 1979.

Included in this dissertation is a discussion and examples of moral dilemmas which do not focus on issues of justice, and which, therefore, pertain to a "broader ethic or valuing process" than the range of moral judgment found in Kohlberg's taxonomy.

Sosevsky, Moshe Chaim, "Incorporating Moral Education Into the Jewish Secondary School Curriculum." Ph.D. dissertation, Ferkauf Graduate School, Yeshiva University, 1980.

Ury, Zalman F. "The Ethics of Salanter and Moral Education in the Jewish School," Ed.D dissertation, University of California, 1966.

Journal

Journal of Moral Education. The NFER – Nelson Publishing Co. Ltd., Darville House 2, Oxford Road East, Windsor, Berkshire SL4 IDF England.

Kohlberg is an associate editor of this journal. It is an excellent source of information on many topics related to moral education.

Audiovisual Materials

"Teacher Training in Values Education: A Workshop." Filmstrip Series, Guidance Associates, 757 Third Ave., New York, NY 10017, 1976.

Kohlberg and Edwin Fenton helped produce this series of four sound filmstrips, which also includes an audiotape, worksheets and a teacher's guide.